THE
BORDERLESS
WORLD

THE
BORDERLESS
WORLD

*Power and Strategy
in the
Interlinked Economy*

Kenichi Ohmae

HarperPerennial
A Division of HarperCollins*Publishers*

This book is dedicated to my friend and colleague, D. Ronald Daniel.

A hardcover edition of this book was published in 1990
by HarperBusiness

First HarperPerennial edition published 1991.

Designed by Ann J. Rudick

**The Library of Congress has catalogued the
hardcover edition as follows:**
Ohmae, Kenichi, 1943
    The borderless world: power and strategy in the
interlinked economy / Kenichi Ohmae.
        p.   cm.
    ISBN 0-88730-473-7
        1. Japan—Commerce—Developing countries.
2. Developing countries—Commerce—Japan.
3. Investments, Japanese—Developing countries.
4. International trade.   5. International economic
relations.   6. Developing countries—Economic policy.
7. Economic development.   8. Economic history—1971-
I. Title.
HF3838.D44043   1990
337—dc20   90-33770

ISBN 0-06-097412-5 (pbk.)
91 92 93 94 95 FG 10 9 8 7 6 5 4 3 2 1

Contents

Preface

One of the lessons I've learned from writing books and articles is that writing about management is safe. But writing about international trade is dangerous. When I published *Triad Power* in 1985, the *Financial Times* called it "one of the most succinct and elegant descriptions of the forces behind the growing globalization of industries and products." A year or two later they 'ran a headline that called me "Japan's Only Management Guru."

But when I wrote about trade issues in *The Wall Street Journal,* things were different. Some of my friends, even a few American colleagues at my consulting firm, McKinsey & Company, worried that I had become an apologist for Japan, that I wasn't being objective about Japan's protectionism and other matters. People even accused me of being an agent for the Ministry of International Trade and Industry.

When in 1983 I outlined in *Japan Business: Obstacles and Opportunities* the many new kinds of alliances and collaborative ventures being formed in autos, electronics, and other industries, some argued that not one of these alliances had worked and that they were really Trojan horses that let the Japanese get into foreign markets. I wasn't believed when I stated in an interview with *Fortune* magazine that the problem for semiconductor manufacturers wasn't the Japanese but the fact that it was becoming a high-fixed-cost, process industry. Yet today Malaysia is the largest exporter of commodity chips.

Why does a nuclear engineer turned management consultant write about trade? It wasn't to defend Japan. I was reacting to forces at work that were becoming very powerful and changing the way our clients operated.

About fifty Japanese companies account for 75 percent of its exports to the United States. My colleagues at McKinsey and I know them very well either as clients or as competitors of clients. As their position has changed, so has the focus of our work as management consultants.

Initially we worked to help develop products, strategies, organizations, people, and management systems. Our goal was to develop good products and sell more for less cost. And if we were successful, our clients would export those products to some overseas countries. But for the most part, our planning horizon did not extend beyond national borders.

The deregulation of the financial markets complicated the situation. After deregulation, corporations could use alternatives to create wealth in key regions of the world in addition to simple manufacturing and selling. To help them gain a market share it was necessary to learn about macroeconomics as well as currency and financial markets.

Protectionism or the threat of it accelerated corporations' efforts to transfer key components of their business systems away from headquarters. That development forced us to think about organization on a global scale and the nature of protectionism itself. I've worked with many large corporations, helping them move from the export-oriented stage of organization to local production and product development, and from the one-headquarters to a four-regional-headquarters model. I have worked with European, American, and Asian corporations to help them establish better and stronger positions in Japan as well. The speed with which the psychology of key managers in these corporations has moved—from local to global, from a nation-based to universal value system, from a headquarters-driven management style to local, market-driven decision making—has been surprising. Words such as overseas operations, affiliates, and subsidiaries are disappearing. Nothing is "overseas" any longer. I was in the right place at the right time to observe impressive groups of managers—not all Japanese—achieve these transitions in a relatively short period.

This book, then, pulls together my understanding and experience of business strategy and competition with my beliefs and analysis of macroeconomic issues. It starts out as a book about strategy and the organization of international companies. Then it attacks the bureaucrats in our governments, who are losing their power but causing great problems on their way out the door. Finally, it begins to describe the economic world toward which we are moving.

By "strategy" I mean creating sustaining values for the customer far better than those of competitors. It therefore means first of all invention and the commercialization of invention. Most people in big companies have forgotten how to invent. They know how to buy and sell businesses or produce me-too products, but they don't develop products that are really better. Nor do they develop new businesses to support these new ideas.

I don't mean just large-scale, high-tech development projects like High Definition Television (HDTV), but products used everyday by most men and women. How do you make a coffeepot, for example, that actually makes better coffee? Or a bubble bath that really is good for your skin? How many product managers staring at their computer screens do you think could do that? Not many. They're too worried about competition and market-share and profitability figures. I believe it's time for big companies to relearn the art of invention. But this time they must learn to manage invention in industries or businesses that are global, where you have to get world-scale economies and yet tailor products to key markets.

Companies have to do that because more informed and demanding customers are coalescing in all developed countries. It is they who really have the power, not the organizations who sell to them. Most people probably don't realize this yet despite the many articles and books on globalization. They still think of giant multinationals forcing their will on people in the countries in which *they choose* to operate. If this book has another purpose besides helping its readers understand the fundamentals of strategy and commercialization, it is to show how multinational companies are truly the servants of demanding consumers around the world. It is these customers who are driving them to operate, develop, make, and sell in many countries at once and who in the process are helping to create a borderless economy where trade statistics are meaningless.

If it does that, you will agree that it is time to throw the bureaucrats out. There is a role for governments—to protect the environment, to educate the work force, and to build a safe and comfortable social infrastructure. When governments are slow to grasp the fact that their role has changed from protecting their people and their natural resource base from outside economic threats to ensuring that their people have the widest range of choice among the best and the cheapest goods and services from around the world—when, that is, governments still think and act like the saber-rattling, mercantilist ruling powers of centuries past—they discourage investment and impoverish their people. Worse, they commit their people to isolation from an emerging world economy, which, in turn, effectively dooms them to a downward spiral of frustrated hopes and industrial stagnation. By looking outward with almost paranoid suspicion, fearing that exploiters will make off with whatever of value they have, they ignore the needs of their people and destroy the value—the human capital—the people represent. In both the political and the economic arena, as recent events in Eastern Europe have shown, the people—as consumers and as citizens—will no longer tolerate this antiquated role of government.

There are bureaucrats in the United States and Japan as surely as there are in Eastern Europe. They miscount the trade figures and get them wrong month after month, and in the process they provide the weapons for economic war between nations. But their time will come too, just as it has for bureaucrats elsewhere.

An isle is emerging that is bigger than a continent—the Interlinked Economy (ILE) of the Triad (the United States, Europe, and Japan), joined by aggressive economies such as Taiwan, Hong Kong, and Singapore.

It is becoming so powerful that it has swallowed most consumers and corporations, made traditional national borders almost disappear, and pushed bureaucrats, politicians, and the military toward the status of declining industries.

The emergence of the ILE has created much confusion, particularly for those who are used to dealing with economic policies based on conventional macroeconomic statistics that compare one nation against another. Their theories don't work anymore. While the Keynesian economist would expect to see jobs increase as an economy picks up, the ILE economy sometimes disappoints them. Jobs might be created abroad instead. If the government tightens the money supply, loans may gush in from abroad and make the nation's monetary policy nearly meaningless. If the central bank tries to raise the interest rate, cheaper funds flow in from elsewhere in the ILE. For all practical purposes, the ILE has made obsolete the traditional instruments of central bankers—interest rate and money supply.

In the ILE most interest-bearing instruments have taken a backseat to noninterest-bearing (and often speculative) instruments such as real estate, stocks, and currency exchange markets. These latter markets have absorbed the enormous excess liquidity produced by vote-buying, deficit-ridden governments, thereby curbing inflation. The ILE is flooded with superliquidity, but thanks to fact that these speculative markets have large buckets, the excess money has been contained and has not done evil (inflation) to ordinary people.

This flow of funds is largely invisible. The traditional way of looking at the trade statistics, based on a nation's balance with another nation, has become obsolete, because ILE residents have learned to move their production and other functions around. Old-fashioned bureaucrats, trying to correct the imbalance figures, make decisions that are comparable to pouring oil on a fire. They create barriers and artificial controls over what should be the free flow of goods and money. Some even try to fix the figures by fiddling with the currency exchange rate. Currency, being the conversion factor of all tradable goods, services, and assets, changes the balance of power within the ILE as wealth thus redistributed is dramatically different from the national economy–based balance of power.

According to the old macroeconomist's view, the exchange rate should change to adjust for the differences in purchasing power of tradable goods and in rates of inflation and interest between the two countries in question. The emergence of the ILE has made this concept obsolete. Assets are now traded across the (old) national boundaries. Companies change hands across borders as easily as paintings, patents, and real estate.

The ILE has a resident body of approximately 1 billion people, enjoying on average $10,000 per capita gross national product. It is in the ILE that most of the wealth in the world is created, consumed, and redistributed. Participation in the ILE is key to prosperity for traditionally isolationist nations. Only through establishment of a healthy two-way pipeline can a developing nation prosper, for the ILE is where nations can get the best value for what they produce. Wealth is now created in the marketplace, rather than in colonies and in soils that contain natural resources.

In this interlinked economy, there is no such thing as absolute losers and winners. A loser becomes relatively attractive as its currency gets weaker and an unemployed work force emerges that is available at reasonable cost. Winners' economies, on the other hand, are adjusted downward toward the mean of the ILE by changes in their currency and wage rates.

Looking into the 1990s and toward the twenty-first century, the ILE is certain to grow faster. It will encompass most East European countries, most of Asian newly industrialized economies (NIEs), and some Latin American countries, if they adopt ILE policies. Interdependencies of economy create security, and that is going to be the governing thought in the ILE as opposed to the military-based security of the Cold War regime.

The policy objective for the ILE will be ensuring the free flow of information, money, goods, and services as well as the free migration of people and corporations. Traditional governments will have to establish a new single framework of global governance. Toward that end, the first and most important step is to understand the global economy accurately. That's the purpose of this book.

People are global when as consumers they have access to information about goods and services from around the world. But these same people could support protectionist representatives if all they read is rhetoric based on archaic nationalistic sentiments. Students, even today, are learning old economic theories that do not work in the ILE. Most of these theories were created at the turn of the century when the national model—the closed economy—was *the* model. Most statistics are still gathered based on this old framework, and hence macroeconomic analyses tell little about what is happening or what will happen in the world, or even in a country.

It is time for us to look at the real economy of an interlinked world. I cannot now propose a new academic theory of economy governing the ILE. What I have done here is to share the perspective I gained over the years working as a practicing consultant, in the hope that readers will appreciate the view and the potential power of the new world, toward which we are heading. Some might be able to articulate a more rigorous economic model to explain the dynamics of the ILE. Some might extract the political implications of the ILE and propose a new regime to govern the world based on today's economic realities, rather than on the old postwar regimes of the United Nations, the Organization for Economic Cooperation and Development, the General Agreement on Tariffs and Trade, the UN Conference on Trade and Development, and even European Community—1992, most of which are based on the Cold War model or on the idea of North-South Clubs.

I will not be surprised if someone comes up with a proposal for a supergovernmental structure, with a taxation system for ILE residents being evenly divided, such as one-third to the world outside of the ILE, one-third to the immediate community in which they live, and one-third to the country. This would reflect the view of the world I've developed over time—as a global citizen, as a resident of my community, and as a Japanese (in that order).

Other readers might find good ideas to develop products, strategies, and organization for the company for which they work. As an author and management consultant, I hope that is where this book's value will be most immediate. I would also like students to read this book before they hear all the old theories and become so fixed in their perspective they cannot see the world as it is and insist on trying to explain everything with the tools they have at hand.

Trying to cover everything from product development to international organization, from currency and trade discussions to developing country issues may seem to be too broad an agenda. However, my feeling is that we need to pull these traditionally isolated subjects together to describe the characteristics of the ILE in a borderless world. My belief is we will accumulate more and more evidence in the 1990s to describe the new ILE that is far bigger than nation-states today, and that we will all gain legitimate citizenship in it before long.

What follows, then, is a prediction or at least a hope that utility will triumph over ideology. It is based on my faith in man as inventor and in the power of informed customers to triumph over man as regulator. It's the regulators we have to fear.

Acknowledgments

There are many colleagues, clients, and friends to thank for their help on this book. They are spread literally all over the world, some well known, others not to most readers. I cannot thank each of them here. I thank Mark Greenberg, the publisher of Harper Business, for his commitment to this book. I would like to acknowledge Professor Theodore Levitt, who persuaded me to write a series of articles on globalization for the *Harvard Business Review*. These articles became the basis of several chapters in this book. Alan Kantrow helped me to organize my ideas and get them on paper. Bill Matassoni gave me, as usual, the right balance and emphasis that this book should have. I thank them all for their help and encouragement.

Finally, I dedicate this book to Ron Daniel. Ron was McKinsey's managing director for twelve years. During his tenure our offices worldwide doubled and McKinsey became a truly global organization with a single set of shared values.

December 1989
Osaka, Japan

1

An Inside-Out View of
Macroeconomics

Despite the time I spend writing and managing McKinsey in
Japan, I still spend most of my time in the field. Day to day I work
with senior managers in all parts of the Triad (the United States,
Europe, and Japan) and Asian newly industrialized economies
(NIEs) to help devise and implement strategies. I've never discovered any formulas or algorithms for getting things right. As I first
described the process in *The Mind of the Strategist*, effective strategies do not result from specific analyses but from a particular
state of mind, a state in which

insight and consequent drive for achievement, often amounting to a
sense of mission, fuel a thought process which is basically creative
and intuitive rather than rational. Strategists do not reject analysis.
Indeed, they can hardly do without it. But they use it only to stimulate the creative process, to test the ideas that emerge, to work out
their strategic implications, or to ensure successful execution of high-
potential "wild" ideas that might otherwise never be implemented.
Great strategies, like great works of art or great scientific discoveries,

1

call for technical mastery in the working out but originate in insights that are beyond the reach of conscious analysis.*

I would not change much of this today. Certain concepts and approaches—strategic degrees of freedom, say, or key factors for success—are of great help in preparing the way for the strategist's creativity. Fact-based analyses of markets and customers and products are, if anything, more important than ever in a world grown more complicated and treacherous. But they are like daubs of color on a palette. They are only the raw material on which "the mind of the strategist" draws.

All textbooks aside, this is still for me the essential, unchanging fact about the hands-on work of building real strategies in real companies. Earlier, however, I argued that good strategies had to comprehend—and strike the right balance among—the three key points of what I called the "strategic triangle" of customers, competitors, and company (an organization's distinctive strengths and weaknesses). Today, as a genuinely interlinked economy emerges, two more Cs have to be added to the list: "country," by which I mean the various government-created environments in which global organizations must operate, and "currency," by which I mean the exposure of such organizations to fluctuations in foreign exchange rates.

So important have these last two Cs become that no responsible company can operate in a borderless environment without paying real attention to them. They are no longer the background against which the findings of a "strategic triangle" analysis get tested. Instead, they belong on the original palette with which strategic minds do their work. When a sudden fluctuation in trade policy or exchange rates can turn an otherwise brilliant strategy into a seemingly irreparable hemorrhage of cash, making arrangements to deal with such fluctuations must lie at the very heart of strategy, not be an afterthought to a strategy defined by other considerations.

*Kenichi Ohmae, *The Mind of the Strategist* (New York, McGraw Hill, 1982), 4.

Customers: Their Emerging Power

You have read enough about "global" products to realize that few of them exist. But there are emerging global market segments; most of them are centered in specific countries. For example, the market for off-road vehicles is centered in the United States, with incremental sales elsewhere. What is important to understand is the *power* of these customers vis-à-vis manufacturers. Part of that power comes from their lack of allegiances.

Economic nationalism flourishes during election campaigns and infects what legislatures do and what particular interest groups ask for. But when individuals vote with their pocketbooks—when they walk into a store or showroom anywhere in Europe, the United States, or Japan—they leave behind the rhetoric and mudslinging.

Do you write with a Waterman or a Mt. Blanc pen or travel with a Vuitton suitcase out of nationalist sentiments? Probably not. You buy these things because they represent the kind of value that you're looking for.

At the cash register, you don't care about country of origin or country of residence. You don't think about employment figures or trade deficits. You don't worry about where the product was made. It does not matter to you that a "British" sneaker by Reebok (now an American-owned company) was made in Korea, a German sneaker by Adidas in Taiwan, or a French ski by Rossignol in Spain. What you care about most is the product's quality, price, design, value, and appeal to you as a consumer. My observations over the past decade seem to indicate that the young people of the advanced countries are becoming increasingly nationalityless and more like "Californians" all over the Triad countries—the United States, Europe, and Japan—that form the Interlinked Economy (ILE).

But this applies to more than just a small segment of consumer products. It is just as true, for example, for industrial customers. The market for IBM computers or Toshiba laptops is not defined by geographic borders but by their appeal to users, regardless of where plants and factories are.

Chip makers buy Nikon steppers because they are the best, not because they are made by a Japanese company. Manufacturers buy Tralfa industrial robots for the same reason, not because they happen to be Norwegian. The same goes for robots made by DeVilbiss in the United States. Companies around the world use IBM's Materials Resource Planning (MRP) and Computer Integrated Manufacturing (CIM) systems to shorten production times and cut work-in-process. Because of the demands of contemporary production, they use Fujitsu Fanuc's control systems and Mazak machine tools made by Yamazaki. In fact, Fujitsu Fanuc dominates the numerically controlled (NC) machine-tool market worldwide: Its market share in Japan is 70 percent; around the globe, 50 percent. This is neither accident nor fashion. These NC machines deliver value through productivity improvement, and everyone knows it.

Governments can still arbitrage information or otherwise protect their markets by forcing citizens to buy high-priced beef (as is the case in Japan) or poor-quality automobiles (the case in India and Brazil), but product labels are spreading all over the world and news of product performance is harder to suppress. Information has empowered consumers. At the same time the position of companies and competitors has been weakened. All this has made the key objective a company's ability to *create new value* for customers (product strategy), not to erect barriers to competitors.

Competition: The Dispersion of Technology

Today's products rely on so many different critical technologies that most companies can no longer maintain a lead in all of them.

The business software that made IBM Personal Computers such an instant hit was not an IBM product. It was the creation of Lotus Development Corporation. Most of the components in the IBM PC itself were outsourced as well. IBM could not have developed the machine in anywhere near the time and cost it did if it had tried to keep it 100 percent proprietary. The heart of IBM's accomplishment with the PC lay in its decision and ability to approach the development effort as a process of managing multiple external vendors.

Lotus provided applications software, and Microsoft wrote the operating system on an Intel microprocessor. Of course, Lotus, Microsoft, and Intel don't want to sell only to IBM. They want to reach as wide a range of customers as possible. Just as IBM needs to rely on an army of external vendors, so each vendor needs to sell to a broad array of customers. The inevitable result is the rapid dispersion of technology. No one company can do it all simultaneously. No one company can keep all the relevant technologies in-house, as General Motors did during the 1930s and 1940s. And that means no company can keep all critical technologies out of the hands of competitors around the globe.

Even original equipment manufacturers with captive technology are not immune to this dispersion. NEC may develop a state-of-the-art memory chip for its own mainframes, but it can sell five times the volume to other computer makers. This generates cash, lowers unit costs, and builds up the experience needed to push the technology further. It also gets the developing company better information about its new products: External customers provide tougher feedback than do internal divisions. To be a world-class producer, NEC must provide the best new technology to global customers, some of them competitors.

Because new technologies become generally available more quickly, time has become even more of a critical element in strategy. Nothing stays proprietary for long. And no one player can master everything. Thus operating globally means operating with partners—and that in turn means a further spread of technology.

Company: The Importance of Fixed Costs

To compete in global markets, companies have to incur—and somehow find a way to defray—immense fixed costs. They can't play a variable-cost game any more. They need partners who can help them amortize their fixed costs, and with them they need to define strategies that allow them to maximize contribution to fixed costs.

As automation has driven the variable cost of labor out of production, manufacturing has increasingly become a fixed-cost activity. And because the cost of developing breakthrough ideas and turning them into marketable products has skyrocketed, research and development (R&D) has become a fixed cost too. In pharmaceuticals, for instance, when it takes $50 million or more to come up with an effective new drug, R&D is no longer a variable-cost game. Moreover, most companies can't even count on being able to license a new drug—a variable cost—from other companies not operating in their primary markets unless they have their own proprietary drug to offer in return. With globalization, all major players in an industry are—or may become—direct competitors. You can't be sure in advance that they (or you) will want to share a particular piece of technology. You need partners, certainly, but you need your own people and your own labels too. That's fixed cost.

In much the same way, building and maintaining a brand name is a fixed cost. For many products, a brand name has no value if brand recognition falls below certain levels. When a company decides to buy a paper copier, for example, it usually calls two or three producers in the order of their brand familiarity. If your copier is not among them, you don't even get a chance to sell your

product. You have to be there to enjoy a high level of aware-
ness among customers. And that means you have to pay for the
privilege.

Trying to save money on brand promotion makes no sense if
what you're selling is a consumer "pull" product: You spend a
little money but not enough to realize any "pull" benefits. A
half-supported brand is worse than no brand at all. With some
products, you can better use the same money to enhance commissions (a variable-cost game) so that the sales force will push them.
In branded competition, if you want to play, you have to ante up
the fixed costs of doing so.

The past decade has seen a comparable movement toward fixed
costs in sales and distribution networks. You can try to play the
variable-cost game by going through distributors, but your sales
force still has to provide the support, the training, and the manu-
als. All of these are fixed costs.

You can also try to make some of these costs variable on your
own. You can chase low-cost labor, for example, by moving
production to developing countries, but that won't get you very
far. In the past, you could make the cost of your computers and
information management systems variable by time-sharing, but
experience has shown that you can't use time-sharing if you want
a system that's dedicated to your own needs and capable of
providing competitive advantage. So, today, information technology is mostly a fixed cost. Over the long term, all these fixed
costs become variable through adjustments in investment (capital
expenditure) levels. But for the short term, they remain fixed.
And so does the need to bolster contribution to them.

This is a fundamental change from fifteen or even ten years
ago. In a variable-cost environment, the primary focus for managers is on boosting profits by reducing the cost of materials,
wages, and labor hours. In a fixed-cost environment, the focus
switches to maximizing marginal contribution to fixed costs—
that is, to boosting sales. This new logic forces managers to amortize their fixed costs over a much larger market base and this
drives them toward globalization.

Another C

Two new Cs or forces now must be considered when formulating strategy. The first is currency. Current exchange rates are much more volatile than they were a decade ago. The yen/dollar rate, for example, has fluctuated between 240 and 120 in the last several years. International companies have tried to neutralize the impact of currency by essentially matching costs to revenue (insiderization) and by becoming strong in all regions of the Triad, so that if one is negative, the others are positive. Companies have taken these steps in addition to traditional measures of moving into low-cost countries, polishing their techniques of international finance (for example, hedging, netting, options), and automation. By doing all of these, most leading-edge companies have succeeded in becoming virtually "currency neutral."

It's not possible to get to a currency-neutral position unless that objective is considered up front when you think about plant utilization, necessary break-even capacity, likely sales by country, and so on. It has to be an objective for international companies as long as currency exchange rates remain volatile. And they will remain volatile as long as government bureaucrats intervene in currency markets armed only with the delusion that changes in the exchange rates can effect companies' export strategies.

The Second C

The second new C is country. Most companies have to move more deeply into the countries where they seek to neutralize the impact of currency as well as the possibilities of protectionism. Moreover, to serve them well, they have to be closer to their customers, at least in the key markets. The commonalities and differences of serving these markets are key ingredients of strategy. Only truly global companies can achieve "global localization,"* that is, be as much of an insider as a local company but still accomplish the benefits of world-scale operations.

The country variable was important to multinationals in the 1960s and 1970s, but then it was basically a matter of assessing a country's political risk and attractiveness in terms of market size/growth and local competition. The main purpose of choosing the country then was to find fertile ground to replicate and clone models of the parent company's products/services. In that sense, multinational enterprises (MNEs) were no different from the Roman Catholic Church's approach to globalization. They pushed their headquarters dogma through the system.

Contemporary global corporations are fundamentally different. They have to serve the needs of customer segments. Instead of educating the "barbarians" to drink Coke or eat cornflakes, they have to discover the basic drinking and eating needs of people and serve these needs. Sometimes they come up with entirely new products and services that headquarters never dreamed of. Coca-Cola's success in Japan was due to the establishment of its route sales forces, but also to its rapid introduction of products unique to Japan. In Japan Mr. Donut's changed everything about its product/service, except for the logo.

The New Multinational Company

The shift in power and changes in these Cs have pushed companies to spread across borders in a new way. The changes have been so rapid that they have outrun the ability of managers to make needed institutional adjustments—companies have been slow to break up nearsighted headquarters and spread their staff more broadly. More important, changes have far outrun compa-

---

*A term coined by Akio Morta of Sony. It is the last of the five-phase development pattern of a globalization process described in my book *Beyond National Borders* (Homewood, IL, Dow Jones-Irwin, 1987).

nies' ability to make more difficult, because less visible, adjustments in underlying assumptions and points of view. Most companies are still nationalistic down deep and see only local customers' needs as well as they need to.

But sooner than most people think, our belief in the "nationality" of most corporations will seem quaint. It is already out of date.

Is IBM Japan an American or a Japanese company? Its work force of 20,000 is Japanese, but its equity holders are American. Even so, over the past decade IBM Japan has provided, on average, three times more tax revenue to the Japanese government than has Fujitsu. What is its nationality? Or what about Honda's operation in Ohio? Or Texas Instruments' memory-chip activities in Japan? Are they "American" products? If so, what about the cellular phones sold in Tokyo that contain components made in the United States by American workers who are employed by the U.S. division of a Japanese company? Sony has facilities in Dotham, Alabama, from which it sends audiotapes and videotapes to Europe. What is the nationality of these products or of the operation that makes them?

These are no longer anomalous situations. They have become commonplace and they will become even more so. As Harvard professor Robert Reich has noted, "The very idea of 'American' products made by 'American' firms is becoming obsolete. Lee Iacocca warns of the Japanese invasion of America, but American-made parts now constitute a smaller portion of the top models of the Big Three than they do of Honda's top-of-the-line cars."*

Most companies in the Triad are still financed by local debt and equity and serve local markets with locally made goods produced by local workers. For them, nationality still has meaning. But for a growing population of firms that serve global markets or face global competition, nationality will disappear.

*"Members Only," *The New Republic,* June 26, 1989.

Government's Role

There is another aspect of the country variable, and that is the role of government, which must change and is changing. Not that long ago, in the "preconsumer" era, "country" was synonymous with a sovereign, isolated island within which its government determined what made most sense to the people who lived there. A government's role was to represent its people's interest, serve their purposes, and protect them from threat of foreigners and foreign corporations. When a country's commercial interests spread outside of its sovereignty, the military was there to back them up. British military forces guarded British interests in the Seven Seas when its plantations were spread all over the world. American forces were fully behind their corporations in the Banana Republic and in the rest of the world to back up the 1960s' and 1970s' multinationalization process. As with the Roman Catholic church, country and doctrine were synonymous, and corporations used overseas countries to provide resources and/or markets to absorb/accept their one-sided, dogmatic, home-grown monolithic products. This is no longer the case. People have become more informed and clever, as a real consequence of living in a truly global information era. And now governments have become the major obstacle for people to have the best and the cheapest from anywhere in the world.

What the energy crisis has taught us is that for a short term the "have" nations can create a supply shortage if they gang up. However, over a longer period of time, alternative supplies develop and the economic principles of supply and demand prevail. If you look at the prosperous nations today—Switzerland, Singapore, Taiwan, South Korea, and Japan—they are characterized by small land mass, no resources, and well-educated hardworking people who all have the *ambition* to participate in the global economy. Having an abundance of resources has truly slowed down a country's development, because bureaucrats there still think that money could solve all problems. In a truly interlinked, global economy, the key success factor shifts from resources to the marketplace, in which you have to participate in order to prosper. It also means *people* are the only true means to create wealth.

As for companies, the prosperity of countries depends on their ability to *create value* through their people, and not by husbanding resources and technologies. While developing countries in particular must learn this lesson, so too must old bureaucrats in the United States, Japan, and the European Community (EC).

In a truly interlinked economy, a country can't fail single-handedly, nor can it win alone. Winning becomes increasingly expensive, as currency and wages are rapidly adjusted and an incremental gain costs dearly in terms of competitiveness. That is the stage Japan and West Germany have entered. Even if a country is outside of the Triad, or the Organization for Economic Cooperation and Development (OECD), or the EC, as long as it can link its economy freely with the rest of the world, it can take advantage of the global economy. Singapore and Hong Kong are doing exactly that. Because neither country has farmers, each has virtually no tariffs on agricultural products. That means people there can buy the best products at the lowest price. The fact that food costs are *cheaper* in Singapore than in Japan because Singapore doesn't produce domestically is a good example of what I am talking about. Even in the isolationist, resource-based economy of Australia, entrepreneurs such as Rupert Murdock and John Elliot (of Elders IXL) can flourish by reaching out to the ILE. Thus the prosperity of the ILE is not only for its residents but for anyone ambitious enough to interlink.

The government's role, then, is to ensure that its people have a good life by ensuring stable access to the best and the cheapest goods and services from anywhere in the world—not to protect certain industries and certain clusters of people. Contemporary governments must become transparent to their people with respect to the rest of the world. Every time governments try to protect resources, markets, industries, and jobs, they cost taxpayers dearly. Only two decades ago when multinational companies had a colonial attitude, they took advantage of the privileges and licenses allotted to them by governments. They were exploitative. But consumers in today's world are much better informed, and the surviving global corporations are there to serve their needs. If they don't, they will be eliminated by the customers, not by the host governments.

Unfortunately, old-style governments still license and regulate foreign corporations to come in and operate. Once they are inside, corporations take advantage of their special position. So we see cars in developing countries whose doors do not shut when slammed, a model that is at least a decade old introduced as a new model, components and spare parts not available, and so on; none of this happens in a truly open market, where competitors eliminate poor performers. Government officials exercise power by regulating and deregulating the market, but their new role is to assume a backseat, not the driver's position, and to make sure that their country is benefiting fully from the best-performing corporations and producers in the world, at the lowest possible cost to their people on a long-term basis.

The Myth of National Security

Under Cold War assumptions, government officials fall back on arguments that countries have to be prepared for emergencies— that is, war. Inefficient industries are subsidized in the name of national security. Even with the Cold War subsiding, government and special-interest groups are still trying to build their cases on these old assumptions. Japan is producing rice, just in case the what if happens. But it is costing its people dearly, in terms of subsidies to farmers and the nation's limited flat land that could be used for housing and pleasure.

Meanwhile, Singapore and Hong Kong don't worry about what ifs. In theory, Singapore can't exist because it has no insurance, either in the form of military forces or strategic (read protected) industries. Yet it enjoys current prosperity. I believe the Singaporean solution is the right one, because in the global economy, economic interlinkage increases security. Nixon's soybean embargo against Japan is often cited as evidence of America's possible clout and Japan's excessive dependence on imported agricultural products. But here again, buyers and markets have the upper hand today. The embargo lasted only a few weeks. Commodity producers need markets, just as developed markets need products. Interlinked and secure supply-demand relationships will have inherent checks and balances. For most commodity suppliers, there are short-term and longer-term alternatives. Soybeans, cotton seeds, and palm oil could all end up being salad oil and detergent. Right-wing politicians in Japan need to recognize this too when they threaten to cut off the supply of advanced chips to the United States. They are ignorant of the fact that more than half of semiconductor production machinery and software to design complicated chips are American made. Moreover, the supply-demand relationships in this industry are much more complex than the right-wingers realize. They know nothing about rare gases, photo resists, and other materials necessary for production—most of which are American controlled. Where there is a market, there will be a producer, and no boycott will last long.

Developed Versus Developing Countries

We tend to think that a country's economy consists of primary, secondary, and tertiary industries. Yet we should now think of the interlinked part of the world as having that spectrum of industries *collectively* instead of individually. This viewpoint really forces the interlinkage into our economic interdependence, and thus there will be no black sheep among us. In this way the people of developing nations can have the products of the developed world at the same price as in the United States, and the developed countries can liberate their taxpayers from having to carry their old industries forever.

A modern government's concern is *jobs.* One of the key reasons for governments' protectionism against foreign products and capital is job security. But what we have observed over the past decade is that this conventional wisdom is wrong. During Reagan's eight years when American imports soared, the United States created more jobs than ever in its history. Japan, forced by its fellow OECD members, has opened one market after another. Unemployment in Japan didn't soar. On the contrary, today the labor shortage is so acute that some people are organizing to import *gastarbeiter,* or foreign workers, from Asian neighbors. Other rapidly growing economies have had the same experience. As markets are liberalized, wage rates go up. The consuming habit caves in, and the economy rapidly shifts to the service sector. The service sector occupies more and more of the total employment. In the United States 70 percent of the work force works in the service sector; in Japan, 60 percent; and in Taiwan, 50 percent. These are not necessarily busboys and live-in maids. They are earning as much as manufacturing workers, and often more. In an interlinked global economy, the fact that primary (agricultural, forestry, fishery) industries slip out of a country and even secondary (manufacturing) industries go overseas is not the end of the world from an employment point of view.

Most governments want foreign producers to come in and build factories. Government officials frequently ask me to help them attract Japanese manufacturers. What they don't realize is that the cost of manufacturing today is typically 25 percent of the end-user price. Production per se adds very little value in the eyes of the customer. It is usually just labor that creates no more value than it costs. Furthermore, the leading-edge producers have all but eliminated simple labor and work from production, and steel-collar workers (robots) do most of the jobs. The "production" such firms have attracted typically consists of watching the robots, quality checks, shipments, and factory maintenance. Countries will gain a lot more important and profitable parts of businesses if they can attract R&D, engineering, financing, and marketing functions. But no government official has ever asked me to bring in those functions.

Governments around the world have tried to protect their markets, industries, and jobs and have failed to do so, because they don't understand the value-added chain in globally interlinked economies. The most value added is in the marketplace today. By opening the market for the most competitive products from anywhere in the world, a country can take advantage of the most opportunities for job creation. Such functions as distribution, warehousing, financing, retail marketing, systems integration, and services are all legitimate parts of the business system and can create as many, and often more, jobs than simply manufacturing operations. Preoccupation with production typically forces governments to hang onto old, incompatible industries and hence do disservice to their taxpayers and consumers (often the same people). Each job thus maintained from the old times discourages the dynamic growth of new industries. There is no need to worry about Tokyo, New York, and Los Angeles becoming service-based tertiary economies, nor to worry about a country becoming a Tokyo or New York. In the interlinked global economy, the producing nation must accept whatever money Tokyoites and New Yorkers use to buy "real" products. That means that the money will come back to buy something from New York or Tokyo, perhaps software, design, technology, real estate, or a brand name. It's no different from a person from California buying a high-rise office building in Manhattan. We are all part of the same interlinked economy.

2

The Equidistant Manager

Even in companies that have operated internationally for years, most managers are nearsighted. Although their competitive landscape often stretches to a global horizon, they see best what they know best: the customers geographically closest to home. These managers may have factories or laboratories in a dozen countries. They may have joint ventures in a dozen more. They may source materials and sell in markets all over the world. But when push comes to shove, their field of vision is dominated by home-country customers and the organizational units that serve them. Everyone—and everything—else is part of "the rest of the world."

No responsible manager purposefully devises or implements an astigmatic strategy. But too few managers consciously try to set plans and build organizations as if they saw all key customers equidistant from the corporate center. Whatever the trade figures show, home markets are usually in focus; overseas markets are not. In fact, words like "overseas," "subsidiaries," and "affiliates" are used to distinguish their home operation from the rest of the world—a symptom seldom observed in a truly global firm.

Not long ago the chief executive officer (CEO) of a major Japanese capital goods producer canceled several important meetings to attend the funeral of one of his company's local dealers.

When I asked him if he would have done the same for a Belgian dealer, one who did a larger volume of business each year than his late counterpart in Japan, the unequivocal answer was no. Perhaps headquarters would have had the relevant European manager send a letter of condolence. No more than that. In Japan, however, tradition dictated the CEO's presence. But Japanese tradition isn't everything, I reminded him. After all, he was the head of a global, not just a Japanese, organization. By violating the principle of equidistance, his attendance underscored distinctions among dealers. He was sending the wrong signals and reinforcing the wrong values.

It may be unfamiliar and awkward, but the primary rule of equidistance is to see—and to think—global first. Honda, for example, has manufacturing divisions in Japan, North America, and Europe—all three legs of the Triad—but its managers do not think or act as if the company were divided between Japanese and overseas operations. In fact, the very word overseas has no place in Honda's vocabulary, because the corporation sees itself as equidistant from all its key customers. At Casio, top managers gather information directly from each of their primary markets and then sit down together once a month to lay out revised plans for global product development.

There is no single best way to avoid or overcome nearsightedness. An equidistant perspective can take many forms. However managers do it, however they get there, building a value system that emphasizes seeing and thinking globally is the bottom-line price of admission to today's borderless economy.

Global Citizens

On a political map, the boundaries between countries are as clear as ever. But on a competitive map, a map showing the real flows of financial and industrial activity, those boundaries have largely disappeared. Of all the forces eating them away, perhaps the most persistent is the flow of information—information that governments previously monopolized, cooking it up as they saw fit and redistributing it in forms of their own devising. Their monopoly of knowledge about things happening around the world enabled them to fool, mislead, or control the people, because only the governments possessed real facts in anything like real time.

Today, of course, people everywhere are more and more able to get the information they want directly from all corners of the world. They can see for themselves what the tastes and preferences are in other countries, the styles of clothing now in fashion, the sports, the life-styles. In Japan, for example, leaders can no longer keep citizens in substandard housing because people now know—directly—how others live elsewhere. The Japanese now travel abroad. In fact, 10 million Japanese travel abroad annually these days. Or they can sit in their living rooms at home, watch Cable News Network, and know instantaneously what is reported in the United States. During 1988 nearly 90 percent of all Japanese honeymooners went abroad. Facts of these kinds are hard to ignore.

So, for the first time in two thousand years, Japanese people are revolting against their government and telling it what it must do for them. This would have been unthinkable when only a small, official elite controlled access to all information.

In the past, there were inefficiencies—some purposeful, some not—in the flow of information around the world. New technologies are eliminating those inefficiencies and, with them, the opportunity for a kind of top-down information arbitrage—that is, the ability of a government to benefit itself or powerful special interests at the expense of the people by following policies that would never win their support if they had unfettered access to all relevant information. A government could, for example, protect weak industries for fear of provoking social unrest over unemployment. That is less easy to do now, for more people have become cosmopolitan and have their own sources of information. They know what such a policy would cost them.

In South Korea students demonstrate in front of the American

Embassy because the government allows the United States to export cigarettes to Korea, which threatens local tobacco farmers. That's what happens when per capita gross national product (GNP) runs in the neighborhood of $5,000 a year and governments can still control the flow of information and mislead their people. When GNP gets up to around $10,000 a year, religion becomes a declining industry. So does government.

At a GNP of $26,000 a year, where Japan is now, things are really different. People want to buy the best and the cheapest products—no matter where in the world they are produced. People become genuinely global consumers. Japan imports beef and oranges from the United States, and everyone thinks it's great. Ten years ago, however, Japanese students would have been the ones throwing stones at the American Embassy. Japanese leaders used to say American and Australian beef was too lean and too tough to chew. But Japanese travelers have tasted it for themselves and learned that it is cheap and good.

Through this flow of information, the Japanese became global citizens, and so must the companies that want to sell them things. Black-and-white television sets penetrated households in the United States nearly a dozen years before they reached comparable numbers of viewers in Europe and Japan. With color television, the time lag fell to about five or six years for Japan and a few more for Europe. With videocassette recorders, the difference was only three or four years—but this time Europe and Japan led the way; the United States, with its focus on cable TV, followed. With the compact disc, household penetration rates evened up after only one year. Now with Music Television (MTV) available by satellite across Europe, there is no information lag at all. New music, styles, and fashion reach all European youngsters almost at the same time they are reaching their counterparts in the United States and Japan. We all share the same information.

More than that, we are all coming to share it in a common language. Ten years ago when I spoke in English to students at Bocconi, an Italian university, most of them listened to me through a translator. Last year they listened to me directly in

English and asked me questions in English. This is a big change. The preparation for economic union in 1992 for the EC has taken place in language much sooner than it has in politics. We can all talk to each other now, understand each other, and governments cannot stop us. "Global citizenship" is no longer just a phrase in the lexicon of futurologists. It is every bit as real and concrete as measurable changes in GNP or trade flows.

The same is true for corporations. In the pharmaceutical industry, for example, the critical activities of drug discovery, screening, and testing are now virtually the same among the best companies everywhere in the world. Scientists can move from one laboratory to another and start working the next day with few problems. They will find equipment with which they are familiar, equipment they have used before, equipment that comes from the same manufacturers.

Drug companies are not alone in this. Most people, for example, believed that it would be a very long time before Korean companies could produce state-of-the-art semiconductor chips— things like 256K NMOS DRAMs. This is not so. They caught up with the rest of the Triad in only a few short years. In Japan, not that long ago, a common joke among the chip-making fraternity had to do with the "Friday Express." Japanese engineers working for different companies in Kyushu, Japan's southwestern "Silicon Island" only 100 kilometers or so away from South Korea, would catch a late flight there on Friday evenings. Over the weekend they would work privately for South Korean semiconductor companies. This was illegal and violated the engineers' employment agreements in Japan. Nonetheless, so many took the flight that they had a tacit gentleman's agreement not to greet or openly recognize each other on the plane. Their trip would have made no sense, however, if semiconductor-related machines, methods, software, and work stations had not already become similar throughout the developed world.

Walk into a capital goods factory anywhere in the developed world, and you will find the same welding machines, the same robots, the same machine tools. Likewise, all trading rooms for stocks, bonds, and currency look identical to the Reuters and Telerates terminals; so much so that the traders switch companies quite liberally. When information flows with relative freedom, the old geographic barriers become irrelevant. Global needs lead to global products. For managers, this flow of information puts a high premium on learning how to build the strategies and the organizations capable of meeting the requirements of a borderless world, or the ILE.

Global Products

You are the CEO of a major automobile company reviewing your product plans for the years ahead. Your market data tell you that you will have to develop four dozen different models if you want to design separate cars for each distinct segment of the Triad market. But you don't have enough world-class engineers to design so many models. You don't have enough managerial talent, or enough money. No one does. Worse, there is no single "global" car that will solve your problems for you. The United States, Europe, and Japan are different markets with different mixes of needs and preferences. As head of a worldwide company, you cannot write off any of these Triad markets. You have to be in each of them, and with first-rate, successful products. What do you do?

If you are the CEO of Nissan, you first look at the Triad region by region and identify each market's dominant requirements. In the United Kingdom, for example, tax policies make it essential that you develop a car suitable for corporate fleet sales. In the United States, you need a sporty "Z" model as well as a four-wheel-drive family vehicle. Each of these categories is what Nissan's president, Yutaka Kume, calls a "lead-country" model—a product carefully tailored to the dominant and distinct needs of individual national markets. Once you have your short list of lead-country models in hand, you can then ask your top managers in other parts of the Triad whether minor changes can make any of them suitable for local sales. But you start with the lead-country models.

According to Mr. Kume:

> With this kind of thinking, we have been able to halve the number of basic models needed to cover the global markets and, at the same time, to cover 80 percent of our sales with cars designed for specific national markets. Not to miss the remaining 20 percent, however, we also provided each country manager with a range of additional model types that could be adapted to the needs of local segments. This approach allowed us to focus our resources on each of our largest core markets and, at the same time, provide a pool of supplement designs that could be adapted to local preferences. We told our engineers to "be American," "be European," or "be Japanese." If the Japanese happened to like something we tailored for the American market, so much the better. Low-cost, incremental sales never hurt. Our main challenge, however, was to avoid the trap of pleasing no one well by trying to please everyone halfway.

What if Nissan had taken its core team of engineers and designers in Japan and asked them to design only global cars, cars that would sell all over the world? Their only possible response would have been to add up all the various national preferences and divide by the number of countries. They would have had to optimize across markets by a kind of rough averaging. But when it comes to questions of taste and, especially, aesthetic preference, consumers do not like averages. They like what they like, not some mathematical compromise. Kume is emphatic about this particular point. "Our success in the United States with Infiniti, Maxima, 240 SX, and Pathfinder—all designed for the American market—shows our approach to be right. It is also encouraging to find that some of these models are quite well received in Japan. But, had we done it in the old way of listening to two countries, we would not have been so clear on the concept development."

In high-school physics I learned about a phenomenon called diminishing primaries. If you mix together the primary colors of red, blue, and yellow, what you get is black. If Europe says its consumers want a product in green, let them have it. If Japan says red, let them have red. No one wants the average. No one wants the colors all mixed together. It makes sense to take advantage of, say, any technological commonalities in creating the paint. But local managers close to local customers have to be able to pick the color.

When it comes to product strategy, managing in a borderless world doesn't mean managing by averages. It doesn't mean that all tastes run together into one amorphous mass of universal appeal. And it doesn't mean that the appeal of operating globally removes the obligation to localize products. The lure of a universal product is a false allure.

Although the needs and tastes of the Triad markets vary considerably, there may well be market segments of different sizes in each part of the Triad that share many of the same preferences. In the hair care market, for instance, Japanese companies know a lot more about certain kinds of black hair, which is hard and thick, than about blond or brown hair, which is often soft and thin. As a result, they have been able to capture a few segments of the United States market in, say, shampoos. That makes an incremental addition to their sales. But it does not position them to make inroads into the mainstream segments of that market.

Back to the automobile example: There is a small but identifiable group of Japanese consumers who want a "Z" model car like the one much in demand in the United States. During the peak season, Nissan sells about 5,000 "Z" cars a month in the United States and only 500 in Japan. Those 500 make a nice addition, of course, generating additional revenue and expanding the perceived richness of a local dealer's portfolio. But they are not the mainstay of such portfolios.

There is no universal "montage" car—a rear axle from Japan, a braking system from Italy, a drive train from the United States—that will quicken pulses on all continents. Remember the way the tabloids used to cover major beauty contests? They would create a composite picture using the best features from all of the most beautiful entrants—this one's nose, that one's mouth, the other one's forehead. The portrait that emerged was never very appealing. It always seemed odd, lacking in distinctive character. But there will always be beauty judges—and car buyers—in, say, Europe, who, though more used to continental standards, find a special attractiveness in the features of a Japanese or a Latin American. So much the better.

For some kinds of products, however, the kind of globalization that Harvard's Ted Levitt writes about makes excellent sense. One of the most obvious is battery-powered products, such as cameras, watches, and pocket calculators. These are all part of the "Japan game"—that is, they come from industries dominated by Japanese electronics companies. What makes these products successful across the Triad? Popular prices, for one thing, based on aggressive cost reduction and global economies of scale. Also important, however, is the fact that many general design choices reflect an in-depth understanding of the preferences of leading consumer segments in key markets throughout the Triad. Rapid model changes during the past decade have helped educate consumers about the "fashion" aspects of these products and have led them to base their buying decisions in large measure on such criteria.

With other products, the same electronics companies use quite different approaches. Those that make stereophonic equipment, for example, offer products based on aesthetics and product concepts that vary by region. Europeans tend to want physically small, high-performance equipment that can be hidden in a closet; Americans prefer large speakers that rise from the floor of living rooms and dens like the structural columns of ancient temples. Of course, the high end of American consumers prefer the European approach. But it is a relatively small segment. Companies that have been globally successful in white goods, such as kitchen appliances, focus on close interaction with individual users; those that have prospered with equipment that requires installation (air conditioners, say, or elevators) focus on interactions with designers, engineers, and trade unions. To repeat: approaches to global products vary.

Fashion-oriented, premium-priced branded goods make up another important cluster of these global products. Gucci bags are sold around the world, unchanged from one place to another. They are marketed in virtually the same way. They appeal to an upper-bracket market segment that shares a consistent set of tastes and preferences. Not everyone in the United States or

Europe or Japan belongs to that segment. But for those who do, the growing commonality of tastes qualifies them as members of a genuinely cross-Triad, global segment. There is even such a segment for top-of-the-line automobiles, such as the Rolls-Royce and the Mercedes-Benz. You can—in fact, should—design such cars for select buyers around the globe. But you cannot do that with Nissans or Toyotas or Hondas. These companies had to create a completely separate image and distribution channels to compete effectively with the "German segment" in the United States, for example, Infiniti, Lexus, and Acura, respectively. Truly universal products are few and far between.

Insiderization

Some may argue that this definition of universal products is unnecessarily narrow, that many such products exist that do not fit neatly into top-bracket segments: Coca-Cola, Levi's, things like that. On closer examination, however, these turn out to be very different sorts of things. Think about Coca-Cola for a moment. Before it got established in each of its markets, the company had to build up a fairly complete local infrastructure and do the groundwork to establish local demand.

Access to markets was by no means assured from day one; consumer preference was not assured from day one. In Japan, the long-established preference was for carbonated lemon drinks known as *saida*. Unlike Gucci bags, consumer demand did not "pull" Coke into these markets; the company had to establish the infrastructure to "push" it. Today, because the company has done its homework and done it well, Coke is a universally desired brand. But it got there by a different route: local replication of an entire business system in every important market over a long period of time.

For Gucci-like products, the ready flow of information around the world stimulates consistent primary demand in top-bracket segments. For relatively undifferentiated, commoditylike products, demand expands only when corporate muscle pushes hard. If Coke is to establish a preference, it has to build it, piece by piece.

Perhaps the best way to distinguish these two kinds of global products is to think of yourself browsing in a duty-free shop. Here you are in something of an oasis. National barriers to entry do not apply. Products from all over the world lie available to you on the shelves. What do you reach for? Do you think about climbing on board your jetliner with a newly purchased six-pack of Coke? No. But what about a Gucci bag? Yes, of course. In a sense, duty-free shops are the precursor to what life will be like in a genuinely borderless environment. The same goods cost the same amount of money no matter what country you are in. In none are prices higher because of duties or taxes. For shoppers, Hong Kong and Singapore are not far from a borderless environment in a larger scale, except for their local residents' life-style. Customer pull, shaped by images and information from around the world, determines your product choices. You want the designer handbag or the sneakers by Reebok, which are made in Korea and sold at three times the price of equivalent no-brand sneakers. And there are others like you in every corner of the Triad.

At bottom, the choice to buy Gucci or Reebok is a choice about fashion. And the information that shapes fashion-driven choices is different in kind from the information that shapes choices about commodity products. When you walk into the 7-Elevens of the world and look for a bottle of cola, the one you pick depends on its location on the shelf, its price, or perhaps the special in-store promotion going on at the moment. In other words, your preference is shaped by the effects of the cola company's complete business system in that country.

The quality of that business system will depend to some extent on the company's ability to leverage skills developed elsewhere or to exploit synergies with other parts of its operations—marketing competence, for example, or economies of scale in the production of concentrates. Even so, your choice as a consumer rests on the power with which all such functional strengths have been brought to bear in your particular local market—that is, on the company's ability to become a full-fledged insider in that local market.

With fashion-based items, where the price is relatively high and the purchase frequency low, insiderization—assembling a complete or near-complete business in the country—does not matter all that much. With commodity items, however, where the price is low and the frequency of purchase high, the insiderization of functional skills is all-important. There is no way to be successful around the world with this latter category of products without replicating your business system in each key market.

Coke has 70 percent of the Japanese market for soft drinks because Coke took the time and made the investments to build up a full range of local functional strengths, particularly in its route sales force and franchised vending machines. It is, after all, the *Coke* van or truck that replaces empty bottles with new ones, not the trucks of independent wholesalers or distributors. When Coke first moved into Japan, it did not understand the complex, many-layered distribution system for such products. So it used the capital of local bottlers to re-create the kind of sales force it has used so well in the United States. This represented a heavy, front-end, fixed investment, but it has paid off. Coke redefined the domestic game in Japan—and it did so not from a distance, but with a deliberate "insiderization" of functional strengths. Once this sales force is in place, for example, once the company has become a full-fledged insider, it can move not only soft drinks but also fruit juice, sport drinks, vitamin drinks, and canned coffee through the same sales network. It can sell pretty much whatever it wants to.

The millions of dollars Coke's competitors, foreign and domestic, are spending on advertising are like droplets of water sprinkled over a desert. Nothing is going to bloom—at least, *not* if that is all they do. Not if they fail to build up their own distinctive "insider" strengths.

When global success rests on market-by-market functional strength, you have to play a series of domestic games against well-defined competitors. You have to become a true *insider* in that market. If the market requires a first-class sales force, you have to have one. If competition turns on dealer support programs, that's where you have to excel. Some occasions *do* exist when doing more better is the right, the necessary, course to follow. Still, there are usually opportunities to redefine these domestic games to your own advantage.

Companies that fail to establish a strong insider position tend to mix up the strategies followed by the Cokes and the Guccis. The managers of many leading branded-goods companies are often loud in their complaints about how the Japanese market is closed to their products. Or, more mysteriously, about the inexplicable refusal of Japanese consumers to buy their products when they are obviously better than those of any competitor anywhere in the world. Instead of making the effort to understand Japanese distribution and Japanese consumers, they assume that something is wrong with the Japanese market. Instead of spending time in their plants and offices or on the ground in Japan, they spend time in Washington.

This is not true of everyone, of course. There are plenty of branded-goods companies that *are* well represented on the Japanese retailing scene—Nestlé, Schick, Wella, Vicks, Scott, Del Monte, Kraft, Campbell, Unilever (its Timotei shampoo is number one in Japan), Twinings, Kellogg, Borden, Ragu, Oscar Meyer, KitKat, and a host of others. These have all become household names in Japan. They have all become insiders.

For industrial products companies, becoming an insider often poses a different set of challenges. Because these products are chosen largely on the basis of their performance characteristics, if the companies cut costs or boost productivity, their products stand a fair chance of being accepted anywhere in the world. Even so, however, these machines do not operate in a vacuum. Their success may have to wait until the companies that make them have developed a full range of insider functions—engineering, sales, installation, finance, service, and so on. So, as these factors become more critical, it often makes sense for the companies to link up with local operations that already have these functions in place.

Financial services products have their own special characteristics. Product globalization already takes place at the institutional investor level, but much less so at the retail level. Still, many retail products now originate overseas, and the money collected from them is often invested across national borders. Indeed, foreign exchange, stock markets, and other trading facilities have already made money a legitimately global product. An interlinked economy has emerged in most financial markets.

In all these categories, then, as distinct from premium fashion-driven products like Gucci bags, insiderization in key markets is the route to global success. Some top-of-the-line tastes and preferences have become common across the Triad, but in most cases creating a global product means building the capability to understand and respond to customer needs and business system requirements in each critical market.

A New Model for Companies Operating Abroad

In the early days of global business, such experts as Raymond Vernon of the Harvard Business School proposed, in effect, a United Nations model of globalization. Companies with aspirations to diversify and expand throughout the Triad were to do so by cloning the parent company in each new country of operation. If successful, they would create a mini–UN of clonelike subsidiaries repatriating profits to the parent company, which remained the dominant force at the center. Now we know that successful companies enter fewer countries but penetrate each of them more deeply. That is why Vernon's model gave way by the early 1980s to a competitor-focused approach to globalization. By this new logic, if we were a European producer of medical electronics equipment, we had to take on General Electric in the United States so that it would not come over here and attack us on our home ground. Today, however, the pressure for globalization is driven not so much by diversification or competition as by the needs and preferences of customers. Their needs have globalized, and the fixed costs of meeting them have soared. That is why we must globalize.

Managing effectively in this new borderless environment does not mean building pyramids of cash flow by focusing on the discovery of new places to invest. Nor does it mean tracking your competitors to their lair and preemptively undercutting them in their own home market. Nor does it mean blindly trying to replicate home-country business systems in new colonial territories. Instead, it means paying central attention to delivering value to customers—and to developing an equidistant view of who they are and what they want. Before everything else comes the need to see your customers clearly. Only they can provide legitimate reasons for thinking globally.

3

Getting Back to Strategy

―――――――――――――――――

"Competitiveness" is the word most commonly uttered these days in economic policy circles in Washington and most European capitals. The restoration of competitive vitality is a widely shared political slogan. The nearness of 1992 and the coming unification of the Common Market focus attention on European industries' ability to compete against global rivals. On both continents, senior managers, who started to wrestle with these issues long before politicians got hold of them, search for successful models to follow. With few exceptions, the models they have found and the examples they are studying are Japanese.

To many Western managers, the Japanese competitive achievement provides hard evidence that a hallmark of a successful strategy is the creation of sustainable competitive advantage by beating the competition. If it takes world-class manufacturing to win, you have to beat competitors with your factories. If it takes rapid product development, you have to beat them with your labs. If it takes mastery of distribution channels, you have to beat them with your logistics system. No matter what it takes, the goal of strategy is to beat the competition.

After a decade of losing ground to the Japanese, managers in the United States and Europe have learned this lesson very well. As a guide to action, it is clear and compelling. As a metric of performance, it is unambiguous. It is also wrong.

Winning the manufacturing or product development or logistics battle is not a bad thing. But it is not really what strategy is—or should be—about. When the focus of attention is on ways to beat the competition, strategy inevitably gets defined primarily in terms of the competition. For instance, if the competition has recently brought out an electronic kitchen gadget that slices, dices, and brews coffee, you had better get one just like it into your product line—and get it there soon. If the competition has cut production costs, you had better get out your scalpel. If it has just started to run national ads, you had better call your agency at once. When you go toe-to-toe with competitors, you cannot let them build up any kind of advantage. You must watch their every move. Or so the argument goes.

Of course it is important to take the competition into account, but that should not come first in making strategy. First comes painstaking attention to the needs of customers and close analysis of a company's real degrees of freedom in responding to those needs. The willingness to rethink what products are and what they do, as well as how best to organize the business system that designs, builds, and markets them, must follow. Competitive realities are what you test possible strategies against; you define them in terms of customers. Tit-for-tat responses to what competitors do may be appropriate, but they are largely reactive. They come second, after your real strategy. Before you test yourself against competition, your strategy should encompass the determination to create value for customers.

It also should encompass the determination to *avoid* competition whenever and wherever possible. As the great philosopher Sun Tzu observed five hundred years before Christ, the smartest strategy in war is the one that allows you to achieve your objectives without having to fight. In just three years, for example, Nintendo's "family computer" sold 12 million units in Japan alone, during which time it had virtually no competition at all. In fact, it created a network of companies working to help it succeed. Ricoh supplied the Zylog chips; software houses produced special games to play on it, such as Dragon Quest I, II, and

III. Everyone was making too much money to think of creating competition.

The visible clashes between companies in the marketplace—what managers frequently think of as strategy—is in reality but a small fragment of the strategic whole. Like an iceberg, most strategy should be submerged, hidden out of sight. The visible part can foam and froth with head-to-head competition. But most is intentionally invisible—beneath the surface where value gets created, where competition gets avoided. Sometimes direct competition cannot be avoided. The product is right, the company's direction is right, the perception of value is right, and managers have to fight it out with competitors. But in my experience, managers too often and too willingly launch themselves into old-fashioned competitive battles. It's familiar ground. They know how to fight. They have a much harder time seeing when an effective customer-oriented strategy could avoid the battle altogether.

The Big Squeeze

During the late 1960s and early 1970s, most Japanese companies focused their attention on reducing costs through such programs as quality circles, value engineering, and zero defects. As these companies went global, however, they began to concentrate instead on differentiating themselves from their competitors. This heavy investment in competitive differentiation has now gone too far; it has already passed the point of diminishing returns—too many models, too many gadgets, too many bells and whistles.

Today, as a result, devising effective customer-oriented strategies has a special urgency for these companies. A number of the largest and most successful face a common problem—the danger of being trapped between low-cost producers in the newly industrialized economies and high-end producers in Europe. While this threat concerns managers in all the major industrial economies, in Japan, where the danger is most immediate and pressing, it has quickly led companies to rethink their familiar strategic goals. As a consequence, they are rediscovering the importance of focusing on customers.

In Japan today the handwriting is on the wall for many industries: The strategic positioning that has served them so well in the past is no longer tenable. On one side, German companies making top-of-the-line products, such as Mercedes or BMW in automobiles, command such high prices that even elevated costs do not greatly hurt profitability. On the other side are such low-price, high-volume producers as Korea's Hyundai, Samsung, and Lucky Goldstar. These companies can make products for less than half what it costs the Japanese. The Japanese are being caught in the middle: They are able neither to command the immense margins of the Germans nor to undercut the rock-bottom wages of the Koreans. The result is a painful squeeze.

If you are the leader of a Japanese company, what can you do? I see three possibilities. First, because Korean productivity is still quite low, you can challenge them directly on costs. Yes, their wages are often as little as one-seventh to one-tenth of yours. But if you aggressively reduce the content of labor in your products, you can close or even reverse the cost gap. In practice, this means pushing hard—and at considerable expense—toward full automation, unmanned operations, and totally flexible manufacturing systems.

Examples prove that it can be done. NSK (Nikon Seiko), which makes bearings, has virtually removed its work force through an extensive use of computer-integrated manufacturing linked directly with the marketplace. Mazak Machinery has taken almost all the labor content out of key components in its products. Fujitsu Fanuc has so streamlined itself that it has publicly announced that it can break even with as little as 20 percent capacity utilization and can export profitably with a currency as strong as 70 yen to the dollar.

This productivity-through-automation route is one way to go. In fact, for commodity products such as bearings it may be the only way. Once you start down this path, however, you have to follow it right to the end with no turning back and no stopping. South Korean wages are so low that nothing less than a total commitment to eliminating labor content will suffice. And China, with wage rates just one-fifth of those in the NIEs, is not far behind South Korea and Taiwan in such light industries as textiles, footwear, and watchbands. Although the currencies of the NIEs are now moving up relative to the dollar, the difference in wage rates is still great enough to require the fiercest kind of across-the-board determination to get rid of labor content.

A second way out of the squeeze is for you to move upmarket where the Germans are. In theory this might be appealing; in practice it has proven very hard for the Japanese to do. Their corporate cultures simply do not permit it. Just look, for example, at what happened with precision electronic products, such as compact disc (CD) players. As soon as the CD reached the market, demand went crazy. Everybody wanted one. It was a perfect opportunity to move upscale with a "Mercedes" compact disc player. What did the Japanese do? Corporate culture and instinct took over, and they cut prices down to about one-fifth of what American and European companies were going to ask for their CDs. Philips was trying to keep prices and margins up, but the Japanese were trying to drive them down. The Western companies wanted to make money; the Japanese instinct was to build share at any cost.

It is clear why the Japanese respond this way. They are continuing to practice the approach that served them well in the past when they were playing the low-cost market entry game that the Koreans are playing now. It's the game they know how to play. But now there's a new game, and the Japanese companies have new positions. The actions that made sense for a low-cost player are way off course for a company trying to play at the high end of the market.

There is another reason for this kind of self-defeating behavior. Sony is really more worried about Matsushita than about Philips, and Matsushita is more worried about Sanyo. This furious internal competition fuels the Japanese impulse to slash prices whenever possible. That's also why it's so difficult for Japanese companies to follow the German route. To do it, they have to buck their own history. It means going their own way and guarding against the instinct to backpedal, to do what their domestic competitors are doing.

Hard as it is, a number of companies *are* going their own way quite successfully. Some, such as Seiko in its dogfight with Casio and Hong Kong–based watchmakers, had been badly burned in the low-price game and are now moving to restore profits at the high end of the market. Others, such as Honda, Toyota, and Nissan in the automobile industry, are launching more expensive car lines and creating second-dealer channels in the United States through which to compete directly for the upscale "German" segment. Still others, such as Nakamichi in tape recorders, have always tried to operate at the high end and have never given in on price. Sony is trying to diversify into the software of the audio-visual (AV) industries, in order to gain more broadly from the industry's total value-added chain and avoid head-on hardware competition with the Japanese AV manufacturers. Such companies are, however, very rare, because instinct runs deep. Japanese producers tend to compete on price even when they do not have to.

For most companies, following the Korean or German approach is neither an appealing nor a sustainable option. This is true not only in Japan but also in all the advanced industrial economies, if for different reasons. What sets Japanese companies apart is the consideration that they may have less room to maneuver than others, given their historical experience and current situation. All these companies have a pressing need for a middle strategic course, a way to flourish without being forced to go head-to-head with competitors in either a low-cost or an upmarket game. Such a course exists—indeed, it leads managers back to the heart of what strategy is about: creating value for customers.

Five-Finger Exercise

Imagine for a moment that you are head of Yamaha, a company that makes pianos. What are your strategic choices? After strenuous and persistent efforts to become the leading producer of high-quality pianos, you have succeeded in capturing 40 percent of the global piano market. Unfortunately, just when you finally became the market leader, overall demand for pianos started to decline by 10 percent every year. What do you do?

A piano is a piano. In most respects, the instrument has not changed much since Mozart. Around the world, in living rooms and dens and concert halls and rehearsal halls, there are some 40 million pianos. For the most part they simply sit. Market growth is stagnant, in polite terms. In business terms, the industry is already in decline; the South Korean producers are now coming on-line with their usual low-cost offerings. Competing just to hold share is not an attractive prospect. Making better pianos will not help much; the up-market has only limited ability to absorb additional volume. What do you do? What can you do?

According to some analysts, the right move would be to divest the business, labeling it a dog that no longer belongs in the corporate portfolio. But Yamaha reacted differently. Rather than selling the business, Yamaha thought long and hard about how to create value for customers. It took that kind of effort—the answers were far from obvious.

What Yamaha's managers did was look—they took a hard look at the customer and the product. What they saw was that most of these 40 million pianos sit around idle and neglected—and out of tune—most of the time. Not many people play them anymore. No one seems to have a lot of time now—and one thing learning to play the piano takes is lots of time. What sits in the homes of these busy people is a large piece of furniture that collects dust. Instead of music, it may even produce guilt. Certainly it is not a functioning musical instrument. No matter how good you are at strategy, you won't be able to sell that many new pianos—no matter how good they are—in such an environment. If you want to create value for customers, you're going to have to find ways to add value to the millions of pianos *already out there*.

So what do you do? What Yamaha did was to remember the old player piano—a pleasant idea with not a very pleasant sound. Yamaha worked hard to develop a sophisticated, advanced combination of digital and optical technology that can distinguish among ninety-two different degrees of strength and speed of key touch from pianissimo to fortissimo. Because the technology is digital, it can record and reproduce each keystroke with great accuracy, using the same kind of 3½-inch disks that work on personal computers. That means you can now record live performances by the pianists of your choice—or buy such recordings on a computerlike diskette—and then, in effect, invite the artists into your home to play the same compositions on your piano. Yamaha's strategy used technology to create new value for piano customers.

Think about it. For about $2,500 you can retrofit your idle, untuned, dust-collecting piece of oversized furniture so that great artists can play it for you in the privacy of your own home. You can invite your friends over and entertain them as well—and showcase the latest in home entertainment technology. If you are a flutist, you can invite someone over to accompany you on the piano and record her performance. Then, even when she is not there, you can practice the piece with full piano accompaniment.

Furthermore, if you have a personal computer at home in Cambridge and you know a good pianist living in California, you can have him record your favorite sonata and send it over the phone; you simply download it onto your computer, plug the diskette into your retrofitted piano, and enjoy his performance. Or you can join a club that will send you the concert that a Horowitz played last night at Carnegie Hall to listen to at home on your own piano. There are all kinds of possibilities.

In terms of the piano market, this new technology creates the prospect of a $2,500 sale to retrofit each of 40 million pianos—not bad for a declining industry. In fact, the potential is even greater because there are also the software recordings to market.

Yamaha started marketing this technology in early 1989, and sales in Japan have been explosive. This was a stagnant industry, remember, an industry that had suffered an annual 10 percent sales decline in each of the past five years. Now it's alive again—but in a different way. Yamaha did not pursue all the usual routes: It didn't buckle down to prune costs, proliferate models, slice overhead, and all the other usual approaches. It looked with fresh eyes for chances to create value for customers. And it found them.

It also found something else: It learned that the process of discovering value-creating opportunities is itself contagious. It spreads. For instance, now that customers have pianos that play the way Horowitz played last night at Carnegie Hall, they want their instrument tuned to professional standards. That means a tuner visits every six months and generates substantial additional revenue. (And it is substantial. Globally, the market for tuning is roughly $1.6 billion annually, a huge economic opportunity long ignored by piano manufacturers and distributors.) Yamaha can give factory workers who might otherwise lose their jobs a chance to be tuners.

As the piano regains popularity, a growing number of people will again want to learn how to play the instrument themselves. And that means tutorials, piano schools, videocassettes, and a variety of other revenue-producing opportunities. Overall, the potential growth in the piano industry, hardware and software, is much bigger than anyone previously recognized. Creating value for the customer was the key that unlocked it.

But what about people's reluctance today to spend the time to learn to play the piano the old-fashioned way? We are a society that prizes convenience, and as the many years of declining piano sales illustrate, learning to play a musical instrument is anything but convenient. Listening to music, as opposed to making music, is more popular than ever. Look at all the people going to school or to the office with earphones on; music is everywhere. It's not interest in music that's going down; it's the interest in spending years of disciplined effort to master an instrument. If you asked people if they would like to be able to play an instrument like the piano, they'd say yes. But most feel as if they've already missed the opportunity to learn. They're too old now; they don't have the time to take years of lessons.

With the new digital and sound-chip technologies, they don't have to. Nor do they have to be child prodigies. For $1,500 they can buy a Klavinova, a digital electronic piano, that allows them to do all kinds of wonderful things. They can program it to play and then croon along. They can program it to play the lefthand part and join in with a single finger. They can listen to a tutorial cassette that directs which keys to push. They can store instructions in the computer's memory so that they don't have to play all the notes and chords simultaneously. Because the digital technology makes participation easy and accessible, "playing" the instrument becomes fun. Technology removes the learning barrier. No wonder this digital segment is now much bigger than the traditional analog segment of the market.

Most piano manufacturers, however, are sticking with traditional acoustic technologies and leaving their futures to fate. Faced with declining demand, they fight even harder against an ever more aggressive set of competitors for their share of a shrinking pie. Or they rely on government to block imports. Yamaha has not abandoned acoustic instruments; it is now the world leader in nearly all categories of acoustic and "techno" musical instruments. What it did, however, was study its music-loving customers and build a strategy based on delivering value linked to those customers' inherent interest in music. It left nothing to fate. It got back to strategy.

Cleaning Up

This is how you chart out a middle course between the Koreans and the Germans and how you revitalize an industry. It is also how you create a value-adding strategy: not by setting out to beat the competition but by setting out to understand how best to provide value for customers.

Kao is a Japanese toiletry company that spends 4 percent of its revenues on fundamental R&D, studying skin, hair, blood, circulation—things like that. (This 4 percent may, at first, sound low, but it excludes personnel cost. This matters because as many as 2,800 of the company's 6,700 or so employees are engaged in R&D.) Recently it developed a new product that duplicates the effect of a Japanese hot spring. A hot spring has a high mineral content and is under extreme pressure. Even the right chemicals thrown into a hot bath will not automatically give you the same effect. Babu, Kao's new bath additive, actually produces the same kind of improvement in circulation that a hot spring provides. It looks like a jumbo Alka-Seltzer tablet. When you throw one Babu into a bath, it starts to fizz with carbon dioxide bubbles as minerals dissolve in the hot water.

Kao's strategy was to offer consumers something completely different from traditional bath gel. Because of its effects on overall health and good circulation, Babu competes on a different ground. In fact, it wiped out the old Japanese bath gel and additives industry in a single year. Now the entire industry has shifted to "hot spring" competition. But the incumbents are having difficulties as they cannot make anything like Kao's product. Kao is playing a different game.

For the new breed of Japanese companies, such as Yamaha and Kao, strategy does not mean beating the competition. It means working hard to understand a customer's inherent needs and then rethinking what a category of product is all about. The goal is to develop the right product to serve those needs—not just a better version of competitors' products. In fact, Kao pays far less attention to other toiletry companies than it does to improving skin condition, circulation, or caring for hair. It now understands hair and skin so well that its newest men's product, called Success, and women's product, called Sofina, fall somewhere between cosmetics and medicine. In that arena, there is no competition.

Brewing Wisdom

Getting back to strategy means getting back to a deep understanding of what a product is about. Some time back, for example, a Japanese home appliance company was trying to develop a coffee percolator. Should it be a General Electric–type percolator? executives wondered. Should it be the same drip-type that Philips makes? Larger? Smaller? I urged them to ask a different kind of question: Why do people drink coffee? What are they looking for when they do? If your objective is to serve the customer better, then shouldn't you understand why that customer drinks coffee in the first place? Then you know what kind of percolator to make.

The answer came back: good taste. I then asked the company's engineers what they were doing to help the consumer enjoy good taste in a cup of coffee. They said they were trying to design a good percolator. I asked them what influences the taste of a cup of a coffee. No one knew. That became the next question we had to answer. It turns out that lots of things can affect taste—the beans, the temperature, the water. We did our homework and discovered everything that affects taste. For the engineers, each factor represented a strategic degree of freedom in designing a percolator—that is, a factor about which something can be done. With beans, for instance, you can have different degrees of qual-ity or freshness. You can grind them in various ways. You can produce different grain sizes. You can distribute the grains differently when pouring hot water over them.

Of all the factors, water quality, we learned, made the greatest difference. The percolator in design at the time, however, didn't take water quality into account at all. Everyone had simply assumed that customers would use tap water. We discovered next that the grain distribution and the time between grinding the beans and pouring in the water were crucial. As a result, we began to think about the product and its necessary features in a new way. *It had* to have a built-in dechlorinating function. *It had* to have a built-in grinder. All the customer should have to do is pour in water and beans; the machine should handle the rest. That's the way to assure great taste in a cup of coffee.

To start you have to ask the right questions and set the right kinds of strategic goals. If your only concern is that General Electric has just brought out a percolator that brews coffee in ten minutes, you will get your engineers to design one that brews it in seven minutes. And if you stick with that logic, market research will tell you that instant coffee is the way to go. If the General Electric machine consumes only a little electricity, you will focus on using even less.

Conventional marketing approaches won't solve the problem. You can get any results you want from the consumer averages. If you ask people whether they want their coffee in ten minutes or seven, they will say seven, of course. But it's still the wrong question. And you end up back where you started, trying to beat the competition at its own game. If your primary focus is on the competition, you will never step back and ask what the customer's inherent needs are or what the product really is about. Personally, I would much rather talk with three housewives for two hours each on their feelings about, say, washing machines than conduct a 1,000-person survey on the same topic. I get much better insight and perspective on what they are really looking for.

Taking Pictures

Back in the mid-1970s, single-lens reflex (SLR) cameras started to become popular and lens-shutter cameras declined rapidly in popularity. To most people, the lens-shutter model looked cheap and nonprofessional, and it took pictures of inferior quality. These opinions were so strong that one camera company with which I was working had almost decided to pull out of the lens-shutter business entirely. Everyone knew that the trend was toward SLRs and that only a better version of the SLR could beat the competition.

I didn't know. So I asked a few simple questions: Why do people take pictures in the first place? What are they really looking for when they take pictures? The answer was simple. They were not looking for a good camera. They were looking for good pictures. Cameras—SLR or lens-shutter—and film were not the end products that consumers wanted. What they wanted were good pictures.

Why was it so hard to take good pictures with a lens-shutter camera? This time, no one knew. So we went to a film lab and collected a sample of some 18,000 pictures. Next we identified the 7 percent or so that were not very good; then we tried to analyze why each of these picture-taking failures had occurred. We found some obvious causes—even some categories of causes. Some failures were the result of poor distance adjustment. The company's design engineers addressed that problem in two different ways: They added a plastic lens designed to keep everything in focus beyond three feet (a kind of permanent focus), and they automated the focus process.

Another common problem with the bad pictures was not enough light. The company built a flash right into the camera. That way, the poor fellow who left his flash attachment on a closet shelf could still take a good picture. Still another problem was the marriage of film and camera. Here the engineers added some grooves on the side of the film cartridges so that the camera could tell how sensitive the film is to light and could adjust. As double exposure was another common problem, the camera got a self-winder.

In all, we came up with some two hundred ideas for improving the lens-shutter camera. The result—virtually a whole new approach to the product—helped revitalize the business. Today, in fact, the lens-shutter market is *bigger* than that for SLRs. And we got there because we did a very simple thing: We asked what the customer's inherent needs were and then rethought what a camera had to be in order to meet them. There was no point slugging it out with competitors. There was no reason to leave the business. We just got back to strategy—based on customers.

Making Dinner

There is no mystery to the process we used, no black box to which only a few gurus have access. The questions that have to be asked are straightforward, and the place to start is clear. A while ago, some people came to me with a set of excellent ideas for designing kitchen appliances for Japanese homes. They knew cooking, and their appliances were quite good. After some study, however, I told them not to go ahead.

What we did was to visit two hundred houses and apartments and take pictures of the kitchens. The answer became clear: There was no room. Things were already stacked on top of the refrigerators. The counters were already full. There was no room for new appliances, no matter how appealing their attributes.

Thinking about these products and understanding the customer's needs, however, did produce a different idea: Build this new equipment into something that is already in the kitchen. That way there is no new demand for space. We were led to the notion of building a microwave oven into a regular oven. Everyone looked at the pictures of two hundred kitchens and said no space. The alternative was to rethink the product.

Aching Heads, Bad Logic

Looking closely at a customer's needs, thinking deeply about a product—these are no exotic pieces of strategic apparatus. They are, as they have always been, the basics of sound management. They have just been neglected or ignored. But why? Why have so many managers allowed themselves to drift so far away from what strategy is really about?

Think for a moment about aching heads. Is my headache the same as yours? My cold? My shoulder pain? My stomach discomfort? Of course not. Yet when a pharmaceutical company asked for help to improve its process for coming up with new products, what it wanted was help in getting into its development pipeline new remedies for standard problems, such as headache or stomach pain. It had assembled a list of therapeutic categories and was eager to match them up with appropriate R&D efforts.

No one had taken the time, however, to think about how people with various discomforts actually feel. So we asked fifty employees in the company to fill out a questionnaire—throughout a full year—about how they felt physically at all times of the day every day of the year. Then we pulled together a list of the symptoms described, sat down with the company's scientists, and asked them, item by item: Do you know why people feel this way? Do you have a drug for this kind of symptom? It turned out that there were no drugs for about 80 percent of the symptoms, these physical awarenesses of discomfort. For many of them, some combination of existing drugs worked just fine. For others, no one had ever thought to seek a particular remedy. The scientists were ignoring tons of profit.

Without understanding customers' needs—the specific types of discomfort they were feeling—the company found it all to easy say "Headache? Fine, here's a medicine, an aspirin, for headache. Case closed. Nothing more to do there. Now we just have to beat the competition in aspirin." It was not easy to take the next step and ask, "What does the headache feel like? Where does it come from? What is the underlying cause? How can we treat the cause, not just the symptom?" Many of these symptoms, for example, are psychological and culture-specific. Just look at television commercials. In the United States, the most common complaint is headache; in the United Kingdom, backache; in Japan, stomachache. In the United States, people say that they have a splitting headache; in Japan it is an ulcer. How can we understand what these people are feeling and why?

The reflex is to provide a headache pill for a headache—that is, to assume that the solution is simply the reverse of the diagnosis. That is bad medicine and worse logic. It is the kind of logic that reinforces the impulse to direct strategy toward beating the competition, toward cutting costs when making traditional musical instruments or adding a different ingredient to the line of traditional soaps. It is the kind of logic that denies the need for a detailed understanding of intrinsic customer needs. It leads to forklift trucks that pile up boxes just fine but do not allow the operators to see directly in front of them. It leads to dishwashers that remove everything but the scorched eggs and rice that customers most want to get rid of. It leads to pianos standing idle and gathering dust.

Getting back to strategy means fighting that reflex, not giving in to it. It means resisting the easy answers in the search for better ways to deliver value to customers. It means asking the simple-sounding questions about what products are about. It means, in short, taking seriously the strategic part of management.

4

Do More Better

Imagine yourself solving an arithmetic problem with the top managers of a leading Japanese automobile company. As a group, Japanese producers already export 2.3 million passenger vehicles a year to the United States. They are also building capacity for an additional 2.5 million vehicles in North America. You remind your friends across the table that the total American market for automobiles is roughly 10 million units a year. How do they expect 4.8 million of them to be Japanese? What adjustments do they anticipate?

For example, do they intend to shut down several of their factories in Japan voluntarily? No, of course not. What Japanese manager wants to be responsible for so much domestic unemployment? Do they think General Motors, Ford, and Chrysler will shut down some of their plants to make room for increased Japanese production? No. Do they intend to use their new North American facilities as rather expensive bargaining chips—cashing them in and closing them down as soon as the United States and Japan negotiate a new trade understanding? Certainly not. Well then, how do they plan to subtract 4.8 from 10 when all the laws of competitive arithmetic say that it won't leave a large enough remainder?

You see, they tell you, there will be more demand for their

company's products. They are going to create a second, demand-boosting marketing channel. And don't forget that they have the plants, the capacity, already in place. They will do just fine, thank you very much. They know how to compete successfully and have the record to show it. Now all they have to do is "do more better." That's not the point, you say. What about the problem of subtracting 4.8 from 10? Not to worry, they answer. The problem, if there is a problem, belongs to somebody else. No, you tell them, the problem is that every "somebody else" is saying the same thing.

The assumption by each Japanese auto company that it can produce and sell an ever-increasing number of vehicles in a market of only 10 million units represents an unwillingness, perhaps an inability, to stand back from particular cases and see the larger, longer-term picture. It also shows a deep-seated inclination to treat all problems as if they belong to somebody else and a commitment to fight every battle to the death. And it leads to a disastrous, company-centered arithmetic, an arithmetic that is ruining industries today.

The Blind Pursuit of Companyism

Many Japanese companies are innovative value-adders. Many others, unfortunately, flunk the arithmetic lesson. For them, the competitive horizon stretches no farther than the end of their own corporate fences. If there is a price to pay for the cumulative effects of their nearsighted decisions, they assume it will come out of someone else's pocket. The logic is simple. The company, after all, must do as it sees fit even if others must pick up the pieces.

Japanese managers are victims of their own success and of the habits that success creates. Not long ago I was talking with the CEO of a large Japanese machinery company who had been an oarsman in college. According to his view of the world, if you want to win, all eight men in the boat bend over a little farther, pull a little harder, work a little better as a team. That's how you beat the other boats. That was his idea of strategy: hunch over and pull harder. No change in course, no pause to look at the distant horizon, no time to take new bearings. If your goal is to beat the competition, you win by narrowing your field of vision and *doing more better.*

In industry as in crew, if the course is perfectly straight and the boat always moves in a true line, this approach makes sense. Pull harder, sweat more, perfect your stroke, work longer hours, and you beat the other guy. Toyota, for example, with its powerful sales force and tremendously innovative engineering group, can afford to focus its manufacturing activities on doing more better. It has the right cars and the right way of getting them to market. So, on the operational side, it can buckle down to the incremental work of cost reduction and quality improvement without allowing its strategic focus to become too narrow.

In today's environment, however, few companies enjoy such well-rounded strengths that they can do more better with impunity. As I argued in the previous chapter, the first principle of strategy is *not* to beat the competition but to deliver value to customers. Delivering value means operating with a keen and flexible sense of direction. Rowing harder does not help if the boat is headed in the wrong direction. Applying more muscle is no solution if the course is mistaken. Getting there quicker is no benefit if the route taken means there are no profits when you arrive. Beating competitors by ruining industries is not strategy.

Yet this is what many Japanese companies have done in industry after industry. They did it in facsimile machines, plain-paper copiers, office automation, watches, color TVs, automobiles, semiconductors, shipbuilding. So *what* if everyone else thinks the same way? We will get ours, and the problem will belong to the other guy. So *what* if this companyism poisons whole industries with rampant overcapacity? So *what* if the resultant price erosion robs the entire industry of profit? In this kind of endurance race, they say, we know how to compete, how to do more better. It has always worked in the past, so why stop now? Back when market growth was unlimited and the course was perfectly straight, their feverish dedication to beating competitors by adding capacity and doing more better worked just fine. It does so no longer. Today foreign markets do not offer boundless, blue-sky opportunities: Japan's very success has given its companies a visibility that attracts attention.

By now the pattern is familiar. Each of the major Japanese semiconductor producers, for example, made three to four times the investment in new capacity warranted by growth in demand during the early 1980s. Each reasoned that if anyone got hurt, it would be the other guy. When orders failed to keep pace, each naturally cut prices to keep its own factories going. This rapid erosion of prices knocked many American and European producers out of the industry entirely. Naturally this brought the U.S. government into the act. Negotiations with the Ministry of International Trade and Industry (MITI) then set a floor under prices, which effectively saved Japanese semiconductor producers from their own folly.

In effect, the two governments created a cartel that guaranteed Japanese producers an adequate price no matter how destructive their investment decisions had been. Today, as demand far exceeds (the "controlled") supply, this cartel gives them unprecedented profits and an unmatched position of dominance. Ironically, the U.S. government, which succeeded in curbing the Japanese onslaught temporarily, has managed to subsidize the Japanese investment in R&D and facilities for the next generation of chips.

Because they did not suffer the consequences of those decisions due to government intervention, Japanese companies will repeat this pattern in one industry after another. They may well do it even if there are negative consequences. Faulty strategy leads them to a short-term focus on beating the competition. Habit keeps them chained to a destructive competitive arithmetic. Profit disappears. And it's always the other guy who's supposed to pay.

The Kabuki of Competition

But why do these companies stick with such devotion to a course that is so obviously self-destructive? Stubbornness is part of it. But, especially in Japan, there is something else. The whaling industry is a good example. Such Japanese companies as Nippon Suisan, Taiyo, and Kyokuyo equipped their ships with the most advanced whale-killing machines and proceeded to kill so many whales that public opinion around the world finally cried out for them to stop. They did not hear the cries because their only real concern was not losing share against their competitors—notably, whalers from the Soviet Union and Norway. Under the 1946 International Whaling Commission agreement, there was free competition up to a predetermined global limit. The more whales you took in a given year, the fewer other whalers could take. No one asked whether so large a catch made sense, whether it might outpace whales' ability to reproduce. Driven by companyism and Olympic Games–like nationalism, no individual company would or could stop—or cut back—on its own.

But they could all quit together: When all lose or all are punished, there is no shame. If all three lose face together, if defeat or retreat is inescapable and affects all alike, then it is acceptable. But if only some companies lose share while others continue to flourish, that is viewed as failure. Voluntarily cutting back on the catch, voluntarily giving up share, is simply not acceptable. Companyism will not permit it. But when the Minister of Agriculture and Fisheries demands that all competitors agree to a scaled-back total catch, that is okay. All competitors are damaged.

There is more. What these companies don't see is that their actions allow the rest of the world to label the entire Japanese population as merciless whale killers. Then the Japanese public interprets the sudden, general attack on them over the whale issue as yet more ill-intentioned "racial lies" against them. In this fashion, excessive companyism can lead to accusations of conspiracy and nationalistic posturing.

It's the same with shipbuilding. Five of Japan's major ship-builders built yards able to build one-million-ton ships. Since Mitsubishi had one, Hitachi and Mitsui had to have one too, and Ishikawajima-Harima Heavy Industries and NKK, and so on. No one could permit competitors to get an edge. The predictable result: gross overcapacity. Everyone started to suffer. And when a group of companies all take the same action as a result of companyism, outsiders may believe there is a national conspiracy to destroy the industry elsewhere in the world. Corrective action was possible only when the pain got bad enough for all of them, when the whole industry began losing share.

It is a Kabuki drama—a highly stylized, exaggerated performance—and even companyism gives way to its logic. Every Japanese knows this, although it's not written down anywhere. When Japanese negotiators go into a bargaining session, they cannot agree to terms right away. They have to go back for a second session and then a third session. Finally, red-eyed and fatigued after many sleepless nights, they can accept at last what they rationally were prepared to accept at the outset. Only when it is clear that they have fought valiantly to the end, when all agree that they could not really have done anything else, can they do what they must.

If management goes into a wage negotiation with a union and comes out a few minutes later with an agreement for a 5 percent increase, the deal cannot possibly last. Everyone will say the settlement was either too high or too low and will fight against it. But if the negotiators lock the door and sit in the room until morning and then stagger out, to announce, grudgingly, that 5 percent was the absolute best they could do under impossible circumstances, then the deal will fly. It's the sheer agony of the struggle that makes the result acceptable. Companyism gets much of its strength from this consensus-building mechanism. Before corrective action is possible, all must suffer visibly.

This is the only way most Japanese have of building consensus in a negative situation. For example, in the recent U.S.–Japan discussions over oranges and beef which resulted in barriers to imports being dropped, the American negotiators looked excessively heroic and the Japanese minister excessively weak. For those who do not know that it is, after all, only a Kabuki drama ("Big Uncle Sam Beats the Poor Japanese All Over the Place"), a completely misplaced sense of nationalism creeps in.

The Benefits of Companyism

Companyism is not just a Japanese disease. Nor must its real-world consequences always prove as destructive as in the semi-conductor and the whaling industries. In fact, Japanese automobile production in the United States might become a good example. By the mid-1990s the survival strategies of these firms based on companyism may make them the largest exporter from the United States. They will not easily lay off their employees and close their plants. They will do their best to make the most out of this initial oversight and collective mistakes by exporting these cars from the United States to all over the world.

Not all companyism is bad. In fact, there is a strong case to be made that many American companies suffer from too little, not too much, companyism. The stockholder-oriented capitalism that today dominates so many American companies places a disproportionate amount of personal wealth in the hands of top-level managers. That is, all members of the company do not share in the economic benefits of the business in anything like an equitable fashion. As a result, the work force is often guilty of too little company loyalty, not too much.

This is understandable. In most Japanese companies, the CEO's total compensation is six to ten times that of the lowest paid factory worker. At Chrysler, Lee Iacocca's $20 million income last year was roughly one thousand times greater than that of his factory workers. Yes, it is the American dream to earn that kind of money, but it also has its downside. So skewed a distribution of privilege and benefit can easily kill the spirit of companyism altogether. Of course, it is dangerous to be blindly loyal to the narrow, short-term interests of your company. But it is also dangerous—perhaps more so—not to care at all, not to feel deeply connected, not to be dedicated.

Where no real vestige of companyism survives, top managers find it easy in a pinch to sell off pieces from the very heart of a business, pieces that should never be sold. Tire companies sell off their tire divisions; machinery companies, their machinery divisions; and aluminum can companies become de facto financial institutions like Primerica. They too easily forget who they are and what business they are in. If times are tough, they'll throw overboard whatever comes to hand. They lack a vital sense of companyism, and their will to stick it out in core business areas is not as strong as it should be.

The stockholders don't really care as long as their money produces more money. In times of need, American companies will sell off their crown jewels—something the Japanese would never do—or, certainly, never do so lightly. At the extreme, the best American company could be a one-person portfolio management operation whose Leveraged Buyout (LBO) funds produce a 30 percent return every year. Amid the blood, sweat, and tears of manufacturing, however, such sweet deals do not exist. Companyism can go too far, but it can also not go far enough.

The Manager's Tool Kit

As mentioned, there are times when hunkering down and rowing harder is precisely the right thing to do. One problem all managers face is knowing when to change course. Another problem is developing a more flexible and far less one-dimensional approach to doing more better—when that is the correct course to follow. Some industry contexts do call for determined, incremental effort, and there is no law that says such effort must be linked to narrowminded definitions of the competitive challenge.

In both cases, the critical issue is the mind-set of managers, their willingness to look at their businesses and their customers' needs with continually fresh eyes. More than their willingness— their insistence. It is human nature to resist change, to stick with what you've got, to do more better of what you know how to do well. But that only makes it more important for managers consciously to refuse to take their business systems or their definitions of customer value as givens. It is their responsibility to rethink those business systems on a regular basis, to take them apart in their minds, to go through a disciplined mental process of decomposing them and then restructuring them from scratch, from a zero-based foundation.

No remedy for the worst excesses of companyism exists, but this kind of zero-based rethinking is a reasonably effective vaccine. Who, for instance, is not aware that IBM means service? Everyone knows it. Everyone values it. Trying to outdo IBM in service or in perceptions of service is a thankless task. Hitachi, a Japanese producer of mainframes, tried a different tack. Perhaps customers are not really interested in service, Hitachi reasoned. Perhaps what they really want is not to need service at all— machines that do not fail, memories that do not evaporate when the power goes out. "No service is good service" is their slogan.

Yoichi Tsuchiya, the president of Sanyo Securities and one of the few CEOs in Japan well versed in computers, once turned off the power supply to all his company's computers. According to Tsuchiya, "Only those made by Hitachi came back on-line quickly when I turned on the power again. The rest either had to go through elaborate procedures or had lost their memories entirely." No point, then, in trying to beat IBM head-to-head at its own game. Much better to rethink what customers really want, as well as the nature of the products that will provide it and the business systems that will deliver it.

It is a question of mind-set. Do managers in your company allow themselves to wonder if their business system needs to be the way it is? Do they give themselves the freedom to rethink it and the products it generates from a zero base? Do they always start such rethinking with detailed attention to customers, or do they concentrate on trying to serve customers with the products, systems, and capabilities now in place? There is an old saying that, to a man with a hammer, all problems look like nails. Do managers in your company think and act as if they had a more varied and extensive tool kit?

Brother, a well-known sewing machine maker, looked at the drop in demand for its products and asked whether its only course of action was to make ever-better sewing machines for a declining market. Not at all, came back the zero-based answer. But you must rethink your business and your customers' needs. What you really know about is not sewing and only sewing. You understand the application of microelectronics to small, precision machines used by operators who make repetitive movements with their hands. Such rethinking led Brother to move quite successfully into typewriters and word processors.

Nor is Brother's transition unique. Textile companies such as Toray have turned themselves into carbon fiber companies. In the United States, Corning Glass Works has become a leading producer of optical fibers, but American copper wire companies have not made the transition from wire to fiber. Not so in Japan. All the leading optical fiber companies there were originally metal wire companies. Yamaha, which had long been active in the motorbike industry, found another use for its expertise with small engines: outboard motors for boats and snowmobiles, where it now holds a 70 percent share of the global market. There are other examples, but the point is clear: Careful thought can often show that doing more better is not the only—or even the most attractive—course of action. In many cases, rethinking the business can lead to doing something *different* that produces a better reward.

Changing to Fit the Changing Customer

Sometimes the need to rethink the business systems grows out of structural changes on the customer side. In Japan, for example, the distribution system for automobiles is quite different from that in the United States. In the United States, you go to a dealer's showroom; in Japan, salespersons come to your door, as if they were selling Avon products. These home sales visits are becoming less efficient, however, because more and more Japanese women are leaving the house to go to work. No one is home during the day.

At the same time, most Japanese adults now have drivers' licenses. They already drive cars. They do not need salespeople to visit them at home with brochures and pictures, because they see all the new models on the streets. The street has become the showroom. In practice, this has meant a shift in the business system—and in labor intensity—from an emphasis on sales to one on service. Dealers now call up their customers to ask if their car is behaving well or to remind them that it is time to get their car serviced or inspected. (After the initial three-year inspection, inspections are mandatory in Japan every two years and are extensive and expensive exercises. The Japanese buy a new car about every five years, and the probability of purchase is greatest just before the second inspection is due.) The dealers even offer to pick up the car for repair and inspection and return it. Maintaining the customer relationship through good service is now the key to success. No showrooms are needed, no door-to-door sales force.

What matters is not any particular solution but rather the determination to escape the reflex of "do more better" and respond to changed conditions by looking at established business systems with fresh eyes. One large mail-order company I worked with was functionally organized into sales, credit approval, and collection, just like all its major competitors. After all, traditional logic said that it was more efficient to specialize and become functional experts. But this approach to organization had its own perverse logic. The sales force sent out catalogs, trying to sell as much as it could. This inevitably led to delinquencies in payment and even defaults because, with such an aggressively expanded sales base, uncreditworthy customers could sneak in. Good sales numbers were not necessarily good numbers for the rest of the organization. It was a vicious cycle.

And it showed. Everyone disliked everyone else. Sales blamed credit approval for getting in its way and blamed collection for making it look bad. Collection blamed sales for generating so many delinquencies. Credit approval couldn't win and resented the beating it took from both directions. It was obviously time to start again from a zero base in thinking about the company's organization and operations.

Our team suggested dividing the country up into areas with roughly one million population and, in each, treating all three functions as a single combined entity that shared a common responsibility for delinquent payments—a single team. Further, we suggested that sales not be counted as sales until the money got collected. It was not very sophisticated, but in a year and a half, earnings improved more than half a billion dollars—without the cry from the top to sell more or collect better.

Accounting According to Human Psychology

In part, escaping the clutches of "do more better" is so hard because it calls on managers to go against firmly entrenched habits. But it is also difficult because most accounting and incentive systems work against it. If you get a close look at a company's accounting system, for example, you ought to be able to guess with fair accuracy how its managers will behave. Top management can override accounting methods, but middle managers can't—they are closer to the customers and are up to their necks in day-to-day decisions. I know of many CEOs who disregard their own systems and tell everyone else in the company to go ahead and do the same. The irony, of course, is that the CEO is the only person in the company who really can afford to follow his own advice.

The sales force of Tokyo Electric Company, an electronic cash-register manufacturer, constantly came up with red bills—red sheets of paper that requested approval for special discounts. It was a chronic problem. Customers would demand this or that special discount or concession, and the salespeople would have to go plead for it, claiming they would otherwise lose the sale. The whole company was constantly divided over these customer demands.

After study, management reorganized the sales effort into a series of three-person teams, each of which had the power to offer whatever special arrangements to customers it wanted. Each operated like a trading company. If a team sold the products at list, it would pocket a 25 percent margin. If it went below list, it would lose the difference. If it sold at a premium, it would pocket the extra yen.

With this new system, salespeople worked around the clock. They also tried to keep the price high because it meant more take-home income. Unproductive discussions between salespeople and their bosses disappeared, and management no longer had to spend precious time approving and disapproving special price concessions. Within a few years the company boosted its overall margins dramatically, and its share of the market went to 42 percent from virtually nothing—all because it had the foresight to change its organization and its accounting and measurement systems in directions based on human psychology.

What you measure and how you measure it have a powerful, often invisible influence on what you think and do. Indeed, in Japan, the absence of effective incentive systems that are tied to strategic performance makes companyism worse. When nothing else gets measured or rewarded, managers will blindly strive to do more better. Companyism is not a synonym for loyalty. It is a reflex, not a purposeful commitment to a company's genuine interests.

Measurement counts. It makes a real difference, for example, if accounting remembers a division's loss this year in its accounts for next year or if the division starts out each year with a clean slate. An accounting system that "remembers" losses product by product is particularly hard on new businesses or on those trying to launch new products. Hitachi has a system like this and has rarely been first to market anything. It is an excellent company, but its accounting system implicitly discourages investment and innovation by its operating divisions. In contrast, Toshiba is much quicker to introduce products because its accounts start fresh each year—a system that tolerates mistakes much more readily.

Incentive systems also tend to get in the way. Most people recognize that in large, divisionalized companies, the pressure on managers is to do more better in order to boost short-term performance. The pressure becomes stronger still when the company is passing through a period of discontinuous change in markets, technologies, or competition. In this kind of unsettled environment, there is a real premium on management's willingness to step back from accustomed ways of doing things and to rethink the whole business system from the ground up. But compensation systems linked to measures of current performance tend to undercut any such willingness. Using incentives to reward doing more better makes sense in some environments but not in all.

Getting back to strategy and focusing on providing value for customers are what lie at the heart of the competitive challenge facing managers today. The need is to build systems that look at a manager's performance over several years, not just on a year-to-year basis. Creating value for customers is a long-term process, and even the time-honored notion of an "annual review" can sometimes get in the way. This, in part, is why the dynamic entrepreneurs who start companies, in both the United States and Japan, are much more likely to carry out a fundamental restructuring of these businesses than any salaried CEO. What successful CEOs do have, however, are much bigger "erasers" than other people—that is, a much greater willingness to let go of what they said yesterday if changes in today's environment, customers, or competitors make it necessary.

The managers' task becomes even more difficult when blind companyism—an unthinking reliance on the principle of sticking to the old and doing more better—is allowed to shape policy or behavior. Konosuke Matsushita, founder of Matsushita Electric Industrial, once told me that his favorite words were *"Torawarenai sunao-na kokoro,"* which means "Mind that does not stick." The need is to look at things with fresh eyes, to rethink approaches from the ground up, to see the opportunities for making money in established businesses and with familiar products. Not every situation requires whiz kids to juggle finances or sketch out restructurings. There are many possibilities for innovation even in old areas of activity.

5

The China Mentality

If you have developed one or two very successful products that have been leaping from the shelves into the waiting arms of consumers, people are going to get lazy. Your sales force will smile and take all the credit for such impressive performance. So will every manager. Salary checks will fatten. Commissions and bonuses will get delivered by the cartload. Some business magazine will run a feature story. All the while, however, far from the limelight, some parts of the company's business system will quietly and steadily atrophy. If experience teaches us anything, it is that success has a thousand fathers—and not one of them minds the baby.

Keeping a company healthy over time means working continually to improve every relevant aspect of its business system. This is not, however, a recipe for tunnel vision or for a knee-jerk determination to do more better no matter what. It is a simple reminder that, in a changeable world, once-and-for-all solutions usually do not work. But neither is there any need to fight the inevitable drift toward habit and laziness by mindless adherence to the established ways of doing things.

Multiple Efforts To Develop New Products

In product development, for example, one tested remedy for complacency is to put in motion several different product teams, provide each of them with the same broad directional guidance, and then let them loose to think up their own approaches to one or another aspect of a common set of problems. That guidance becomes self-defeating, of course, if it is too rigid. No matter how many groups you have, the chances of success will not measurably increase if you ask them all to follow the same Soviet-style five-year plan.

The point, after all, is to generate multiple approaches, multiple solutions, for managers to choose among. That is why such companies as Sharp, Casio, and NEC, for example, have *hundreds* of different projects under way in the area of office automation. Some will die along the way. But the products that result will be all the better. Equally important, these companies will be able to offer customers not a single solution to their needs but several. And the companies will be able to keep their product pipeline aggressively churning out new introductions at regular intervals. Competitors may bring something new to the market every year or two. NEC does it nearly every month.

An organization's culture, the soil in which its managers have to root all their efforts, can prevent such multiple seeds from growing. This will happen inevitably if the managers responsible for the solutions not chosen get criticized, penalized, or ignored. Indeed, many of the companies justly famed for their sustained ability to innovate make a conscious effort to acknowledge and reward these also-rans. But it will also happen if the culture understands product development not as an activity that can— and should—lead to an abundance of possibilities for later choice or exploration but as an activity that, from the outset, screens all possibilities for the one approach that is to be followed. In practice, this means loading the development effort with so many specifications, conditions, and requirements that only one solution is possible.

Companies that take this latter course will argue that development is a very expensive activity. More than that, its costs escalate geometrically the farther along it goes. As a result, they simply cannot afford to keep multiple approaches going for very long. What this argument misses is the fact that much of this cost escalation is driven not by the necessary technical work itself but by the need to follow elaborate corporate protocols, guidelines, and reporting systems. In Japan, where suppliers that are immune to the red tape of a large corporation's R&D department perform many of these technical activities, costs for the same body of technical effort are usually much lower than in the United States. The bureaucratic overhead is missing.

There are four additional problems with this kind of thinking. First, it assumes that each approach will take roughly the same amount of support. Second, it incorrectly calculates how much support for a proposed solution is too much by treating resource allocation as being linked to a single product rather than to a whole series of products and extensions and variants. Third, it puts so great a burden on making the right choice early that everyone gets uptight and the energy for creative solutions dissipates. And fourth, if there is to be only one "answer," then pressure mounts for it to include a wider and more complex range of features than any one product should have to bear. Worse, this pressure also drives the specifications for these features back toward a kind of global average. And as I argued earlier, customers do not want an average solution; they want something that will meet their particular needs.

There is a still deeper problem with the one-solution approach. It sends the wrong organizational message. Remember, a major concern here is the natural tendency of managers to grow comfortable with the status quo. A major new product development is likely to upset the established order of things and to shake things up considerably. But if the culture regards the development as a major, one-time shift, if it is allowed to make even uncomfortable changes in the belief that, once made, they will soon give rise to a new, settled order, then the war has been lost even if the immediate battle has been won. Nothing kills pent-up vitality more swiftly or more effectively than the establishment of a new orthodoxy. The energy for reform has been spent, and the allure of comfort stifles whatever remains of the urge to be different, to innovate.

Hard-headed managers, faced by stiff competition, might be tempted to look these facts in the eye and still say, Okay, we hear you. But no matter how troublesome the side effects of following a one-solution approach, we cannot do otherwise. In a different world, we could allow ourselves the luxury of keeping multiple efforts alive, but the brute reality is that money is tight, time is short, and we just cannot afford to divide our resources or energy or attention. This too is plausible, but it is dangerously wrong.

Or at the least, it is shortsighted. It mortgages the future by emptying the pipeline of all but a single effort. It also risks the sluggishness or, worse, the paralysis that comes with a new orthodoxy. But even these burdens might be worth the risk if this Christmas-tree approach were able to deliver as promised. It cannot. Experience shows that weighting a development effort down with an overly elaborate grab bag of requirements stretches the process out and adds to its cost. Things do not speed up or get less expensive. There is so much testing to be done, so many subdevelopments to coordinate, so many features to combine with each other—that is, so much complexity to manage—that everything takes longer and costs more. Many American corporations seek to emulate the success of the Manhattan Project and the Apollo Project; hence, they tend to have elaborate and expensive R&D processes.

By contrast, running simple but multiple projects may look inefficient from a distance, but it does not have to be. Staff size can be small; the average life of each separate project can be short (at NEC, for example, projects average less than half a year); and the work of coordination can be kept to a minimum. You want these projects to be autonomous. You don't want them to have to spend all their time forging linkages with a dozen different functional groups. What you do want is for each of them, lightly burdened, to go ahead as fast as it can. Of course, there may be redundancy in what these teams do. But if they move quickly enough, that hardly matters. The savings in time more than pays for itself.

What really counts, though, is the value such multiple efforts can deliver to customers. Average products really do fail. The market really does not want a single solution. Some people want a stand-alone word processor. Some want their word processor to contain a facsimile function as well. Some want their facsimile combined with a phone and their word processor with a printer. Some want the boxes on their desk to be taller but thinner. But others do not.

When a company gets used to thinking of its products in a certain way over a long period of time, it can easily lose sight of what customers really want. A useful antidote to this sort of creeping numbness is to go through an explicit, deliberate process of resegmenting the market. This is especially valuable to do when efforts to meet customers demands have created a complicated and varied mix of products.

In Japan, for example, people used to use soap to wash their whole bodies, including their hair. Then came shampoo and, after that, rinse for the hair. Next, of course, there were shampoos for each different type of hair—dry, oily, and so on—and for dandruff. It got to the point that a family had to keep ten or more separate bottles in the bathroom to suit each member's special needs. So today the most attractive product is a combination of shampoo and rinse in a single bottle. This makes life simple. A resegmentation of the market uncovered the value of moving against the tide of ever-increasing market fragmentation.

Another example: Consumer demand in Japan for leading-edge stereo equipment pushed manufacturers to create systems with so many knobs and dials that people finally got confused. It was too much. So now there are stereos with just two knobs: "best sound" in a given acoustic ambience and "volume." It's easy. Unless you pay close attention to gradual shifts in what customers want, you may well miss the opportunity to integrate—to resegment—and, instead, continue to proliferate choices that create little ultimate value. This is not the kind of question you can ever settle once and for all. The answer changes over time. You have to keep asking it and making adjustments.

Do you want broad but narrow representation in the market? Do you want to go wide but shallow? You have to keep experimenting. You can carry out these experiments without having to give anything up. You don't need to eliminate the old products until you find out that the resegmented ones are a hit with consumers. Even better, these experiments tend to create a kind of "Hawthorne effect" in sluggish and mature product categories. By trying things out in new combinations, you can often rekindle consumer interest. Adding rinse to shampoo gets people to *think* about shampoo again. Producing a stereo with only two knobs does the same with music systems.

As always, the challenge is to identify—and respond to—the ever-changing mix of consumer preference. But if you want to be like the military and push all these requirements into a single project, you have to proceed the way the military does: slowly, painfully, cautiously, sluggishly moving ahead across a front so broad that terrain and enemies multiply beyond any organization's ability to count or respond.

Operating like the military puts an immense priority on the sheer bureaucratic work of coordination and logistics. Necessarily so. Paper multiplies. Meetings proliferate. Conferences become endless. Everyone has to check with everyone else before anyone can do anything. Wearing out your bottom in briefing sessions is worth it if the right equipment gets to the right place at the right time. But in their product development work, companies do not have to operate the way armies do. The competition in which they are engaged is like real warfare only to limited extent. They can have flatter command structures. They can take and hold important new positions with only a tiny group of people. They can travel quickly, and they can travel light.

The vision that guides development companies can throw away their advantages by dissipating effort in too many fragmented initiatives. Someone has to have a sense of the overall program, a mental map of the segments that can reasonably be served, a clear idea of which solutions—if they pan out—will find useful applications. But this "someone" does not need to be an elaborately staffed coordinating committee with its own offices and budget and stationery and business cards. It does not have to exert octopuslike control of every conceivable support activity.

Indeed, in many of the leading Japanese companies, this "someone" is, literally, a single individual—a Mr. Honda, a Mr. Kume at Nissan—with a general, shaping vision of what needs to get done and great personal gusto for encouraging the troops and cheering them on. Leaders of this sort have curiosity. They always seem to have two or three ideas about the major problems that need to be solved and how, perhaps, to solve them. They have a vision of the general direction in which things have to move.

For example, back when Mr. Honda was first thinking about how to get his company into the market for passenger cars (instead of their traditional motorcycles), he gave a lot of attention to the environmental consciousness that was just beginning to make itself felt as a social issue. He told his engineers: What we have to have is a vehicle that does not pollute. You eat some food and take a drink and then, sooner or later, you have to go to the bathroom. You leave your waste behind, and then someone has to clean it up. That's a messy and unpleasant business. Well, what we need to do with these vehicles is not produce any waste in the first place. (Actually, what he told his engineers is that they had to find a way to take care of their own piss and shit. This is the expression that got their attention.) All of a sudden, they realized the challenge was not to get more horsepower or more torque or more rpms. It was not even how to use converters and filters to muzzle dirty engines. It was to make the engines themselves clean.

Once good people understand what the vision is, what the concept is, they can set about looking for multiple solutions. If, instead, they have to start with a Christmas-tree list of requirements, there is no way those specs can be defined at the top. They have to come, bottom-up, from the engineers at the bench. So they will lack vision. Only by luck will they even aim in the right direction. And if your people are good, what you will then get is great work, great precision, in the wrong direction. You will get work that is defined by a technical agenda, not work that is directed toward providing value to customers. And those agendas will be defined, in turn, by entrenched assumptions—and by the fierce delight of engineers in doing more better.

Preparing the Soil

In cases such as these, however, human nature also gets some help. Even where vision does exist at the top and does get communicated throughout a product development organization, many things can keep it from being acted upon. Worse still, many things can so water down the response that the organization can fool itself into believing that it is doing what it should when, in fact, it is not.

Think, for a moment, about the silent effects of established measurement systems. Say the top-level vision is clear. What, then, is likely to keep an R&D group from taking multiple approaches to exploring it? Well, for one thing, fear of being seen to incur excessive costs—at least, as costs usually get accounted for. But this makes no sense. In most such efforts, materials and tools account for only a small portion of development expense. The major item is personnel, and the number of people in the affected group is pretty much fixed. It makes no real difference if you divide up, let's say, twenty-one people into three groups of seven or seven groups of three—not in terms of cost. You can, of course, play games with the allocation of overhead that makes a larger number of projects seem inefficient. But that's what they are—games. Most of the time, as every manager knows, these allocations are done by rote, according to a standard formula that usually bears no relation to what really is going on. But if these are the numbers that get reviewed, then these are the numbers to which the people who allocate R&D effort will inevitably pay attention.

But the problem goes beyond the difficulties of allocating costs to specific projects. You cannot account for R&D as if it were a form of business activity just like any other. It is a trial-and-error process in which, by definition, well over 90 percent of what even the best people do is a failure. That's the way they learn. That's the way they narrow down the area for investigation. Applying to such an activity the accounting conventions developed for routine, established management processes (where, in fact, they don't work all that well either) is foolish precision. Product development is not something that incurs specific, focused costs and with which specific revenue streams can later be associated. It is a general investment for the future at a certain level of risk. It would make the people in green eyeshades happier if they could draw up mini–income statements and balance sheets for each project, but their happiness does not matter.

The problems companies face in getting product development effectively hooked up to a shaping vision vary greatly. For some, the flow of good ideas substantially outpaces the understanding of customer needs and market potential. For others, the need and promise are clear, but the idea flow is inadequate. No a priori "correct" approach or solution exists because no two company-specific situations are exactly alike.

At Nissan, for example, product development languished for many years because the internal process gave too strong a voice to the marketing people. With consumers around the Triad snapping up new Toyota and Honda offerings, the marketing boys could always be heard complaining that the products they were being asked to sell were not what the market wanted. If you would give us products like Honda and Toyota are making, they said, we will reverse our drop in share in a moment. Because share had been dropping, the product development people had nothing much to say in return. The pressure was irresistible, and "me too" became the order of the day.

This was not an answer. Much as I argued earlier, competitor-oriented strategies are not a good place to start. At best, you go head-to-head and cut each other's margins. At worst, you are forever trying to catch up. Nissan decided that what it needed to do was not to look at its competitors but to take a fresh look at the market, to see which segments really did make sense, and to target design efforts against them. It adopted a new motto, "Be Thyself," and even started a company bulletin with that name. This is what it has done over the past several years, and the results speak for themselves.

Other companies—several in the computer industry come to mind—may have paid too little attention both to what competitors were doing and to what customers really wanted. The point is that development needs are not the same from company to company. Bottlenecks in the development process do vary.

What this means, in practice, is that the ground for effective development efforts must be prepared differently in different companies—and even in different parts of the same company. At a major pharmaceutical company with which we worked, for example, a falling off in performance directed management's attention toward an unacceptably slow pace of product development in recent years. Why had this happened, they wanted to know, and what could be done about it? The head of R&D saw nothing surprising here. At best, he knew, it takes many years to come up with a new drug formula and define the range of its activity. And it takes many more to test it for toxicity, side effects, and the like. The recent slowness was predictable. It was the nature of things in the drug business.

We were not satisfied. "Who are your best development people?" we asked. "That's not the right question," came the response. "Creating new drugs is a group process. We have some twelve hundred people in our company and, if we are lucky, we bring out five new drugs a year. What you want to know is which are our best groups." We still were not satisfied. "Who are your best people?" we asked again. They didn't know. So we had them identify their twenty-five most profitable drugs then on the market and go back through their records and find out who had come up with the original formula first. Many people had played a critical role in their development, but we wanted to know who had come up with the original idea. It turned out that, of the twenty-five drugs, five had been initially defined by each of two people. Now, two people responsible for ten out of twenty-five drugs in a company of twelve hundred scientists and engineers did not strike us as a random distribution.

"Where are these people now?" we asked. One of them had become a supervisor and was very successful in bringing along new people and supporting their work. The other was in trouble. He had been given some people who reported to him, and he hated it. He ignored and antagonized them. In fact, he antagonized almost everyone he dealt with. So he had the people taken away from him, got penalized in terms of salary and promotion, and was stuck off in a corner of the laboratory feeling miserable and not terribly motivated to do great work. When we first spoke with him, he even agreed that he belonged off in a corner. He felt like a failure and accepted the justice of being treated like one.

This made no sense to us. Here's a man responsible for nearly half the company's profit, and the lab is set up in such a way that he has been rendered useless because he's not good at something—managerial work—that he had never pretended to be good at. Why not treat him like a queen bee? we thought. Why not keep him out of all the regular development groups but make him the expert, the experienced hand, who gets brought in to help solve critical problems when any of those groups gets stuck? He was truly brilliant in a right-brained kind of way. His mind did not seem to operate by strict logic. Instead, it was able to form a holistic picture of the question under study and, thus, identify where focused work should be targeted. He made a perfect complement to the cadres of left-brained, logical scientists who filled out most of the development teams.

Putting these two men in an identical work environment—that is, giving them precisely the same charter—was foolish. It was management by rote, by averages. It was harmful and unnecessary. These two R&D heroes should both be able to function successfully in the same laboratory—if, that is, their differences are recognized and accommodated.

Multiple cultures ought be able to coexist in a development organization. Part of it, no doubt, will need to focus on catch-up or cost reduction or doing more better. Part of it will need to focus on supporting the longer-term strategic plans of the business. But part of it should focus on wild-card activities, on things that—if they work out—would represent major breakthroughs or major changes in the way business is done. Personally, I'm quite aggressive about this division of effort. I like to see budgets divided roughly one-third, one-third, and one-third. It's good for the company. It's also good for the people. Scientists and engineers do not all have a single, shared temperament. Some prefer working on incremental improvements toward a carefully defined goal. Others do not. That's human nature too.

Uncorking the Bottleneck

A Japanese manufacturer of kitchen appliances had a drafting room for its engineers as well as a test kitchen for them to use. When they wanted to understand what their ideas and approaches might mean for customers, they walked from one room to the other. Or they had market survey companies go out and ask consumers whether they would like this or that feature—a garbage disposal in the sink, a garbage disposal that made less noise. Some of these questions were impractical. Disposals, for example, were a nonstarter because Japanese municipalities will not allow them to be installed—the sewage systems in place cannot handle them. When it came to dishwashers, however, the R&D people already knew the answer—or thought they did. First of all, Japanese housewives will never use them until they become as devoted to convenience as Western housewives. Moreover, dishwashers will never be very attractive in Japan until they do a better job of cleaning dishes.

Now, the first of these beliefs was pure prejudice—and wrong at that. Japanese housewives really did like the idea of such convenience. And once the problem of space had been solved (see chapter 2), they were quite enthusiastic about them. But the second belief had merit. Western dishwashers did not work well in Japan. In fact, their performance was terrible. Japanese families eat lots of rice, and scorched rice on a plate or egg glazed on a plate does not come off easily.

What we did, first, was to spend a lot of time trying to understand when and how people actually cleaned dishes in the home. We found that housewives did not put dishes into the machine with the idea that they would use them immediately after they came out. What most of them did was to leave the dishes in the machine until the next day and then either put them away or put them back on the table. In other words, the speed of the dishwashing cycle was largely irrelevant. That meant a slow "soak" cycle could be added to the dishwasher's operation, a period of three hours or so in which the scorched rice and glazed egg would have to loosen up. We even went to a company that specialized in surface chemistry and had them devise a liquid detergent that was ideal for this soak cycle.

The value-added here was to recognize that the company had not been asking the right questions. Its development work on dishwashers had reached a bottleneck because of consumer resistance to a long track record of poor performance.

This is not, however, the only place in which such bottlenecks can occur. In my work with a camera company and with several producers of office machines, for example, I found that the bottleneck lay in their relative lack of attention to issues of aesthetic design. High-performance machines that looked ugly simply did not appeal. The companies had lost touch with what their customers really wanted.

Losing touch is easy to do because it is so easy to do bad market research. Much of the time, as most everyone recognizes, managers ask—or cause to be asked—the kinds of questions that will tell them what they expect to hear. In fact, questions and the statistical analysis of answers is precisely the wrong place to start. First you have to take a mental journey through the area you want to explore. You have to learn everything there is to know about it, and you have to learn it firsthand. If you are studying washing machines, that means you have to spend several weeks watching people wash clothes, asking them what kinds of problems they are having, asking them to explain why they do what they do. You have to get all this in your head—before you start forming the questions to test the hypotheses derived from your observations.

Some may say, for example, that their machine annoys them because it catches fluffy material. Others are bothered because they have no way of knowing when the cycle is finished. Still others may be annoyed that big items, such as sheets and pants, get so wrinkled they have to spend time ironing them. After a while you begin to hear the same comments over and over. They begin to fall into distinct clusters. The people who live in tiny apartments with very little space may agree on one set of complaints. Bachelors with their own homes may agree on another. Now what you've got is a set of inductively derived hypotheses to test, a tentative segmentation scheme that you can probe through market research, focus groups, telephone surveys, and the like.

What you've also got is something you can tell your engineers. You have a list of problems for them to address. Many people are worried about the amount of water their machines use during the rinse cycle. How do we reduce that cycle? Others are troubled about wrinkling. Can we redesign the agitator rod or rethink the whole process of stirring? What can we learn by going back to the principles of supersonic vibration? What other options are there?

Another example: A Western company wanted to sell its fried potatoes in Japan. Its managers were troubled because all their market research—and all the conventional wisdom—told them that Japanese did not eat fried potatoes. This struck me as odd because there are McDonalds and Kentucky Fried Chickens all over Japan, and Japanese children eat the french fries there as avidly as kids do in the States. Something did not add up.

So we visited a number of schools and arranged to spend a few minutes asking the children some questions. What time do you get home? we wanted to know. What time is dinner? Do you get hungry? What do you have for a snack? The list of things was not surprising—candy, chocolate, potato chips, things like that. We also asked what they would really like to eat if they could. Fried potatoes. The problem was not with the children, then, but with the mothers. So we asked them what they didn't like about fried potatoes. Well, they thought of it as a side dish and not as a snack. They thought it was too greasy and messy. But most of all, they were afraid of having the children anywhere near potatoes getting fried *in hot oil.* But the product we were concerned with was already fried. It just needed to be heated up. Well, the mothers knew that too, come to think of it. What really bothered them was the thought of their kids heating them up over an open flame (only about 20 percent of Japanese kitchens have ovens). They did not want them anywhere near fire.

Many kitchens had microwave ovens, but microwaves would not work with the product. What about toaster ovens? we wondered. How would the mothers feel about that? They didn't mind; there was no open flame. We tried them, and it worked okay. The company had to redesign its packaging, but its product was basically fine. In fact, its sales—in what everyone thought was a dead market—tripled in half a year.

The Center of the Universe

Part of what is necessary for a world-class development operation is the ability and the interest—and the courage—to keep asking the question "Why?" until the answers are basic enough to guide creative effort. Not being satisfied with surface explanations of things is an essential ingredient of all truly productive R&D. By this I don't mean giving vent to a pale curiosity but to a visceral need to know the answers to what I have called elsewhere the "five whys"—why, why, why, why, why. This is what it takes to get to the heart of things.

Why, then, do good development people, well-trained professionals, usually stop short? The answer is simple: They don't think they are the center of the universe. They don't have the China mentality—the deep, inner certainty that they can change the world, that if anyone does change the world they will be the ones. This is not the same thing as the NIH (not invented here) syndrome that often gets in the way of productive development work. NIH sufferers can't be bothered to examine or apply good ideas that originate elsewhere. By contrast, the China—*Chu-goku,* literally, means "center of universe"—mentality provides the confidence to look at things in a new light and to push beyond the usual answers to get at underlying causes and connections. It is a source of motivation, and its effects are *in*clusive. NIH is a source of self-satisfaction, and its effects are *ex*clusive.

When development people lack the China mentality, they are not certain that they are true innovators or that, if they have innovated once, they can do it again. Their minds and characters—and the culture that supports both—do not have that flush of elitist self-confidence that says: We alone will really get to the bottom of things, understand them when others have not, and use that understanding to build and create anew. In personality some of them may be arrogant. But deep under the skin, they do not genuinely believe they are the center of the universe.

Not having the China mentality, they are not extremists, not fundamentalists. Not being sure they can change the world, they stop with average answers, half-done attempts to meet customer needs that are themselves but half-understood. Nothing drives them toward extreme levels of understanding of those needs or of the physical laws relevant to them. Lacking this fundamental confidence, they really do not want to know too much because they really do not want to be led to answers that deviate very far, if at all, from the norm. If they go boldly where competitors fear—or do not think—to tread, they run the risk of being wrong, of making mistakes. But if they stay close to the norm, although the benefits will at best be marginal, at least there will be no errors. A fearful, risk-avoiding incrementalism is the product of minds that lack inner confidence.

When you don't believe you sit at the center of the universe, you don't think of yourself as the person who must go listen to hundreds of housewives talk about how they clean dishes or clothes. You don't intuitively know that you should be the one to ask hundreds of children what they like to eat after school. Nothing drives you to do this because you lack the certainty that, if you don't change the world, no one else will. What matters to you is what other people will say or if they will snicker behind their hands. But you can't really care about that. You can't worry about whether people might think you're crazy or whether scholarly opinion will write you down as a lightweight fool or whether your managerial colleagues will keep detailed notes, the better to say I told you so. You cannot care.

For years, we in Japan copied Western products. First we went to the library to see what everyone else thought. Then we looked at what our competitors did. We made reference checks and more reference checks. What confidence we had was limited to the hard-won belief that we could take these established ideas and make them better, faster, and cheaper. But we never thought we could have such ideas ourselves. At the fundamental level, we never thought we also sat at the center of the universe. Happily, this is changing.

A turning point in my own life came during my graduate education at MIT. One of my professors called me into his office to answer some questions. "Tell me," he said, "what you think." My response was to promise to go to the library and get back to him in a day or two. "Nothing doing," he answered. "Use the blackboard right here, and work it out for yourself. If you and I, here in this office, cannot solve this problem, then no one else can. We both know the theory and the most likely approaches. We don't have to look elsewhere. We can solve it ourselves. Here's the chalk."

I hesitated. I didn't know very much about the particular field in question. I wanted to go see what I could find in the library. But that was not his style. He would write down everything he knew that was relevant to solving the problem at hand. He would then write down what he needed to know. If it turned out there was a gap, he might go to the library—but on day five, not day one. This is what he taught me. Don't look elsewhere to see what everyone else thinks. Think for yourself.

Have the confidence that you, unaided, can do it, because that is the only way you will avoid putting your feet precisely where everyone else has gone before. There is no Keep Out sign at the center of the universe. Global players must have the engine and knowlege to propel themselves. They must be directly familiar with the key markets. That knowledge is the secret of success in the borderless world.

6

Getting Rid of the Headquarters Mentality

By all reasonable measures, Coke's experience in Japan has been a happy one. More often than not, however, the path it took to insiderization—replicating a home-country business system in a new national market—creates many more problems than it solves. Managers back at headquarters, experienced in only one way to succeed, are inclined to force that model on each new opportunity that arises. Sometimes it will be the right answer. But chances are that the home-country reflex, the impulse to generalize globally from a sample of one, will lead efforts astray.

In the pharmaceutical industry, for example, Coke's approach would not work in Japan. Foreign entrants simply have to find ways to adapt to the Japanese distribution system. Local doctors will not accept or respond favorably to an American-style sales force. When a doctor asks a local detail man to take a moment to photocopy some articles for him, he *has* to be willing to do so.

One common problem with insiderization, then, is a misplaced home-country reflex. Another problem is what happens back at headquarters after initial operations in another market really start paying off. When this happens, in most companies everyone at home starts to pay close attention. Without really understanding why things have turned out as well as they have, managers at headquarters take an increasing interest in what is going on in Japan or wherever.

Functionaries of all stripes itch to intervene. Management decides it should monitor key decisions, ask for timely reports, take extensive tours of local activities. Every power-that-be wants a say in what has become a critical portion of the company's overall operations. When minor difficulties arise, no one is willing to let local managers continue to handle things themselves.

A cosmetics company with a once-enviable position in Japan went through a series of management shake-ups at home. As a result, the Japanese operation, which had grown progressively more important, was no longer able to enjoy the rough autonomy that made its success possible. Several times eager American hands reached in to change the head of activities in Japan, and memos and phone calls kept up a steady barrage of challenges to the unlucky man who happened to be in the hot seat at the moment. Relations became antagonistic, profits fell, the intervention grew worse, and the whole thing just fell apart. Overeager and overanxious managers back at headquarters did not have the patience to learn what really worked in the Japanese market. By trying to supervise things in the regular "corporate" fashion, they destroyed a very profitable business.

This is a familiar pattern. The local top manager regularly changes from a Japanese national to a foreigner, to a Japanese, to a foreigner. Impatient, headquarters keeps fitfully searching for a never-never ideal "person on the spot." Persistence and perseverance are the keys to long-term survival and success. But headquarters is just not able to wait for a few years until local managers—of whatever nationality—build up the needed rapport with vendors, employees, distributors, and customers. And if, by a miracle, they do, then headquarters is likely to see them as having become too "nationalized" to represent their interests abroad. They are no longer "one of us." And if they do not build up this rapport, then obviously they have failed to win local acceptance.

This headquarters mentality is not just a problem of bad attitude or misguided enthusiasm. These would be relatively easy to
fix. Instead, it rests on—and is reinforced by—a company's entrenched systems, structures, and behaviors. Dividend payout
ratios, for example, vary from country to country. But most global companies find it hard to accept low or no payout from
investment in Japan, medium returns from Germany, and larger
returns from the United States. The usual wish is to get comparable levels of return from all activities, and internal benchmarks
of performance reflect that wish. Looking for a 15 percent return
on investment a year from new commitments in Japan is going
to sour a company on the country very quickly. The companies
that have done the best there—the Coca-Colas and the IBMs—
were willing to adjust their conventional expectations and settle
in for the long term.

Or, for example, when top managers rely heavily on financial
statements, they can easily lose sight of the value of operating
globally—because these statements usually mask the performance of activities outside the home country. Accounting and reporting systems that are parent-company dominated—and
genuinely consolidated statements are still the exception, not the
rule—merely confirm the lukewarm commitment of many managers to global competition. They may talk about doing business
globally, but it is just lip service. It sounds nice, but when things
get tough, most of the talk turns out to be only that.

If a divisionalized Japanese company such as Matsushita or
Toshiba wants to build a plant to make a component in Tennessee, the home-country division manager responsible for that
component often is in a tough position. No doubt the CEO will
tell him to get that Tennessee facility up and running as soon as
possible. But the division manager knows that when the plant
does come on-line his own operations are going to look worse on
paper. At a minimum, his division is not going to get credit for
American sales that he used to make by export from Japan. Those
are now going to come out of Tennessee. The CEO tells him to
collaborate, to help out, but he is afraid that the better the job he
does, the worse it will be for him.

Why not change company systems? Have the Tennessee plant report directly to the manager and consolidate all widget-making activities at the divisional level? Because it's easier said than done. Most companies use accounting systems that consolidate at the corporate, not the divisional, level. This is traditional corporate practice. And every staff person comes fully equipped with a thousand reasons not to make exceptions to time-honored institutional procedures. As a result, the division manager is going to drag his feet. The moment Tennessee comes on-line, he sees his numbers go down, he has to lay off people, and he has to worry about excess capacity. Who is going to remember his fine efforts in getting the Tennessee plant started up? More to the point, who is going to care—when his Japanese numbers look so bad?

If a company wants to operate globally, it has to think and act globally, and that means challenging entrenched systems that work against collaborative efforts. Say the manufacturer in this example has a change of heart and goes to a division-level consolidation of accounts. This helps, but the problems are just beginning. The American managers of a sister division that uses these components looks at the Tennessee plant as just another vendor, perhaps even a troublesome one because it is new and not reliable. Their inclination is to treat the new plant as a problem, ignore it if possible, and continue to buy from Japan where quality is high and delivery guaranteed. They are not going to do anything to help the new plant come on-line or to plan for long-term capital investment. They are not going to supply technical assistance or design help. All it represents is fairly unattractive marginal capacity.

If we solve this problem by having the plant head report to the division manager, then we are back where we started. If we do nothing, then this new plant is going to struggle. Clearly, what we need is to move toward a system of double counting of credits, so that both the American manager *and* the Japanese division head have strong reasons to make the new facility work. But this runs afoul of our entrenched systems, and they are very hard to change. If our commitment to acting globally is not strong, we are not going to be inclined to make the painful efforts needed to make it work.

Under normal circumstances, these kinds of decisions are hard to reach. It is no surprise that many of the most globally successful Japanese companies—Honda, Sony, Matsushita, Canon—have been led by a strong owner/founder for at least a decade. These leaders can override bureaucratic inertia; they can tear down institutional barriers.

In practice, the managerial decision to tackle organizational and systems changes is made even more difficult by the way in which problems become visible. Usually a global systems problem first comes into view in the form of local symptoms. Rarely do such problems show up where the real underlying causes are.

Troubled CEOs may say that their Japanese operations are not doing well, that the money being spent on advertising is not paying off as expected. They will not say that their problems are really back at headquarters, with its superficial understanding of what it takes to market effectively in Japan. They will not say that it lies in the design of financial reporting systems. They will not say that it is part and parcel of their own reluctance to make long-term, front-end capital investments in new markets. They will not say that it lies in their failure to perform well in the central job of any headquarters operation: the development of good people at the local level. Or, at least, they are not likely to. They will diagnose the problems as local problems and try to fix them.

Top managers are always slow to point the finger of responsibility at headquarters or at themselves. When global faults have local symptoms, they will be slower still. When taking corrective action means a full, zero-based review of all systems, skills, and structures, their speed will decrease even further. And when their commitment to acting globally is itself far from complete, any motion is unlikely. The headquarters mentality is the prime expression of managerial nearsightedness, the sworn enemy of a genuinely equidistant perspective on global markets.

Decomposing the Center

No company can operate effectively on a global scale by central-izing all key decisions and then farming them out for implemen-tation. It doesn't work. The conditions in each market are too varied, the nuances of competition too complex, and the changes in climate too subtle and too rapid for long-distance manage-ment. No matter how good they are, no matter how well sup-ported analytically, the decision makers at the center are too far removed from individual markets and the needs of local customers.

Moreover, sitting at world headquarters breeds a nearly irre-sistible—and often fatal—impulse to manage by averages. Do we want an automobile that will sell in worldwide markets? Fine, let's add up all segments' preferences and then divide by the number of segments. From world headquarters, this often seems a plausible, resource-sensitive approach.

The limitations of a single "world" headquarters are not just theoretical but the lesson of experience. For years, an American-based multinational addressed its markets in the Far East from its international division, which was located down the road from its corporate headquarters. The head of Japanese operations had to make twenty pilgrimages a year to get approval first for his an-nual plans and later, when market conditions back home went through inevitable fluctuations, for his revisions of those plans.

The inflexibility of these arrangements did nothing to stop a decline in Far East market share. It may even have accelerated the decline. The only way the top manager in Japan could report acceptable numbers back home was to redefine who the competi-tion was. With each report, more and more companies got removed from the denominator of the market-share calculation. What seemed internally consistent was externally inconsistent. In effect, headquarters demanded that management in Japan re-main faithful to previous plans rather than respond to the chang-ing day-to-day realities of the marketplace.

The company finally recognized that this approach made no sense. At great cost, it moved its international headquarters from the United States to Tokyo, along with its key people. Now the head of Far East activities makes only a few trips a year to the States, and he has the freedom to solve local problems locally. It is no surprise that the division's performance has turned around and its profits have soared; its global decision making is closer to its customers.

This new approach to regional headquarters is not an isolated discovery. Nissan, Yamaha, Sony, Honda, Omron, and Matsushita, among others, have decentralized responsibility for strategy and operations to each of the Triad markets, keeping only the corporate service and resource allocation functions at world headquarters. In fact, the real quantum jump in this direction comes when a company separates its domestic operations from its global headquarters, which can then sit at an equal managerial "distance" from each of the regional Triad headquarters. These companies have recognized that they cannot keep their ablest managers at home. They must send them where the critical action is.

Decomposing the corporate center into several regional headquarters is becoming an essential part of almost every successful company's transition to global competitor status. It is a trend that is consistent with recent developments in Europe as it moves toward economic union in 1992, in North America as it moves toward 1999 (the U.S.–Canada free trade agreement), and in Asia, where the economies of the newly industrialized countries are rapidly integrating with Japan's. This move toward regional headquarters is also consistent with companies' growing need to hedge exposure to currency fluctuations through sound operating decisions and not simply through shrewd use of financial instruments.

By becoming, in effect, an insider in key markets, a global corporation can make its costs independent of home-country currency—that is, at a par with those of domestic competitors in each of its markets. But it can also pull the trick of using cheaper sources of inputs from elsewhere in the world, something local players cannot easily duplicate. The strength of a global corporation derives in no small measure from its ability, as a full-fledged insider, to understand local customers' needs. At the same time, it can deploy human, financial, and technological resources on a global scale.

A Question of Identity

Effective cultivation of global markets requires more than the removal of absentee landlords. Decomposing inevitably creates its own problems. The more successful a company is at bringing both operational and strategic responsibility down to the regional or local level, the more likely it is that local or regional concerns, attitudes, affinities, and allegiances will shape the decisions of its far-flung managerial cadre. As the rulers of the old colonial empires learned, when you send officers to new territories across the ocean, you had better be sure that they have deeply internalized not only the official policies but also the values of the home government. Indeed, the more you try to coordinate and facilitate from the center, the more important the value system your people take with them becomes.

Maintaining a corporate identity in a global environment is different. Formal systems and organizational structures can help, but only to the extent that they nurture and support intangible ties. Training programs, career-path planning, job rotation, companywide accounting, evaluation systems that are equitable across national borders, and electronic data-processing systems become more important as globalization proceeds. The most important, however, is a system of values that all employees in all countries and regions unquestionably accept. A global company must be prepared to pull out of a region where its core values cannot be implemented.

Konosuke Matsushita, the founder of Matsushita Electric Industrial, aspired to serve customers all over the world. In fact, he expected no repatriation of profits and instead kept investing in the national markets he entered. In some of the countries where he wanted to sell color television sets, for example, a high-quality broadcasting system did not exist. So he donated an entire broadcasting station to the local government to improve the picture quality that would be available to his customers. It did not matter to him whether those customers were in overseas markets or in Japan. His dedication to serving them remained the same. It was "good business."

A global corporation today is fundamentally different from the colonial-style multinationals of the 1960s and 1970s. It serves its customers in all key markets with equal dedication. It does not shade things with one group to benefit another. It does not enter individual markets for the sole purpose of exploiting their profit potential. Its value system is universal, not dominated by home-country dogma, and it applies everywhere. In an information-linked world where consumers, no matter where they live, know which products are the best and cheapest, the power to choose or refuse lies in their hands, not in the back pockets of sleepy, privileged monopolies like the earlier multinationals.

Commonly held beliefs can immunize managers against "going native." Their real significance, however, is as counterweights to the growing centrifugal forces that pull managerial actions and decisions from their proper orbits. The more dispersed your people and the closer the attention they must pay to local customers and markets, the more they need to escape the center's rigidities while retaining its shaping values.

Colonial administrators—and early global managers—in the old, pyramidal organizations had only crude means to help their people strike an appropriate balance. For the most part, they used brute force: Distance and poor communication softened rigidity, and the threat of penalty reinforced shared values. Today brute force is neither necessary nor effective. A new form of organization, organic and amoebalike, makes that balance easier to achieve.

This kind of organization represents the final, fifth stage of the process by which companies move toward a genuinely global mode of operation. The first stage is the arm's-length export activity of essentially domestic companies, which move into new markets overseas by linking up with local dealers and distributors. In stage 2, the company takes over these activities on its own. Next comes stage 3, in which the domestic-based company begins to carry out its own manufacturing, marketing, and sales in key foreign markets. In stage 4, the company moves to a full insider position in these markets, supported by a complete business system including R&D and engineering.

Stage 4 calls on managers to replicate in a new environment the hardware, systems, and operational approaches that have worked so well at home. It forces them to extend the reach of domestic headquarters, which now has to provide support functions, such as personnel and finance, to all overseas activities.

Getting to stage 5, however, means venturing onto new ground altogether. To make this organizational transition, companies must denationalize their operations and create a system of values shared by company managers around the globe to replace the glue a nation-based orientation once provided. The best organizations operate in this fashion and, as a result, devote much of their "corporate" attention to defining personnel systems and the like that are country neutral. In a genuinely global corporation, everyone is hired locally. No matter where individuals in an amoeba-like structure are, they can communicate fully and confidently with colleagues elsewhere. Building this level of trust takes time because building shared values takes time. You can try to speed things up by asserting policies and mandating values, but it does not work. Not surprisingly, few if any companies have learned how to operate entirely in such a fashion, but the signs of movement in this direction are numerous and unmistakable.

My own firm, McKinsey, has long experimented with this form of global organization. The center provides only a few "corporate" functions. All of our work with clients around the world is carried out through a network of offices and entrepreneurial individuals, connected to each other by crisscrossing lines of communication rather than lines of authority. These multiple linkages make possible the dissemination throughout our firm of important new learning in any one part of it. Equally important, these linkages mean that creative work can happen—and be recognized and celebrated—anywhere in the network. There is competition in the sense that all our professionals want to provide exceptional value for clients, but there is no conflict because no one instance of first-rate performance detracts from or makes less likely or less visible any other. What holds this network together is our shared sense of identity, which is supported in turn by our commitment to a shared set of values.

Global Integration

For many companies, even—perhaps especially—those with decades of international experience, it has been difficult to move beyond the headquarters-dominated form of multinational organization. Habit dies hard. Headquarters, after all, was where the critical decisions got made; headquarters was the center of the universe. Local subsidiaries might have been closer to customers, but they were distinctly second-class citizens. Their purpose was to serve headquarters by providing it with cash flows, and they got back in return whatever resources the managers at the center thought they should have. No one imagined that headquarters should serve them even though they did the critical work of delivering value to customers. Corporate language reflected these realities. No matter how multinational a company's lines of business, there were "domestic" operations (in the home country, of course) and "overseas" operations (everywhere else).

As companies moved progressively through the stages of evolution just described, little arose to challenge directly their center-focused orientation. Even in stage 4, where companies establish a full "insider" position in key national markets, there was no need to change orientation. Experience showed that it was possible to replicate a complete business system in each of these markets without calling the traditional role of headquarters into question. This remains true today, as many Japanese companies are entering stage 4 in order to finesse both currency fluctuations and the political uncertainties of protectionism in the United States and in the European Community. Fujitsu, for example, is now committed to building a complete business system in the United Kingdom, clean room and all, for its semiconductor operations. NEC has been there for some time. These are major developments, but they do not depart from the familiar logic of multinational organization.

Moving to stage 5, however, is another matter entirely. A company's ability to serve local customers in markets around the globe in ways that are truly responsive to their needs as well as to the global character of its industry depends on its ability to strike a new organizational balance. What is called for is what Akio Morita of Sony has termed global localization, a new orientation that simultaneously looks in both directions. What makes this orientation so difficult to achieve is not so much the organizational complexity it requires. The real difficulty is that the challenge cannot adequately be met, cannot even be held at bay, by redrawing structural charts, no matter how complex they are. At base, the problem is psychological, a question of values.

All through stage 4, remember, the headquarters mentality continues to dominate. Different local operations are linked, their relation to each other established, by their relation to the center. In fact, in most early stage 4 companies, headquarters is responsible for both domestic and overseas operations, often treating the latter as a kind of afterthought and providing them with support functions, such as R&D or personnel or systems, initially tailored to domestic requirements. Even in late stage 4 companies, such as Remy Martin, which have separated domestic from global headquarters and even located them in different buildings, the emphasis is still on running the separate national pieces of a multinational enterprise by linking them to each other through the center.

In stage 5, however, the pieces are linked, individual to individual, not through the center but through a shared set of values. Before national identity, before local affiliation, before German ego or Italian ego or Japanese ego—before any of this comes the commitment to a single, unified global mission. You don't think any longer that the company you work for is a Japanese automaker trying to build and sell its products in the United States. You work for Honda or Nissan or Toyota. The customers you care about are the people who love your products everywhere in the world. Your mission is to provide them with exceptional value. When you think of your colleagues, you think of people who share that mission. Country of origin does not matter. Location of headquarters does not matter. The products for which you are responsible and the company you serve have become denationalized.

Many companies have been able to operate successfully around the world without ever making the transition to stage 5. Coca-Cola, for example, is a multilocal company that is still dominated by a headquarters orientation. However far-flung its operations and however localized its activities, it is an American company. Join the company in Spain, and your frame of reference is the Spanish operation and, beyond that, decisions that get made in Atlanta. If you meet a peer from Japan who does the same job you do, you cannot be certain that you share a common training or language or outlook. You might both share an opinion about things going on in Atlanta, but that is really the only place your experiences connect.

This approach has served Coca-Cola exceptionally well. It suits the nature of its business. But it will not work equally well for the growing list of companies facing genuinely global, not just multilocal, challenges. For them, it is a serious problem if a new manager in Spain has little in common with a French or a Japanese or a German counterpart. For them, it matters that such managers do not, for the most part, even speak each other's language. Quite literally, global firms must share a common language, English, in addition to all the languages spoken locally. I know of two German companies that have recently changed their official language of business from German to English for just this reason. Talent must be accessible around the world. In stage 5, mother-country identity must give way to corporate identity.

Moreover, it's not just the official language of business that must be shared in common around the world; so must the corporate "language"—the unofficial culture of the organization. If you grow up in the same mother-country environment with a managerial colleague, you know from the first few words the other person says when you bump into him or her in a hallway just how things are. You can tell whether something is wrong. If you hear a certain tone of voice or if you miss a certain verbal cue, you can sense it. Nothing needs to be said directly. Nothing needs to be written down. But you know for a fact that you ought to rearrange your calendar and invite your colleague for lunch or dinner or a drink or, perhaps, just to drop by your office later for an informal conversation.

There is no way to manage a genuinely global enterprise, an amoebalike network organization, without shared languages of this sort. And there is no way to develop them quickly. You get to know people, develop confidence in them, learn to read between the lines of what they say only by spending time together, growing up together. You cannot share a working language with them by reading the same manual or going to the same one-shot training program. You have to deal with them, time after time, over a period of years. More than that, you have to come from the same professional world that they do, even though you work for the most part in different countries. If your normal frame of reference is the limited context of your local environment, your worlds will rarely touch or will touch only superficially. Your frame of reference, therefore, must also include, day to day, the universal values you share with your colleagues in every part of the world.

If it does not, stage 5 will remain an elusive goal. Imagine, for example, that the head of your operations in Spain, a Spanish national, is a quirky man who has always delivered in terms of performance. Imagine further that he does not really share your company's informal language. As long as things go well, no one bothers him all that much. No one looks over his shoulder too closely. You may be uncomfortable with what he is doing or how he is doing it, but you respect his track record and so leave him alone. As soon as the numbers do not look the way they should, however, the temptation will be irresistible to be all over him. You will not give him the room you would give your colleagues elsewhere with whom the cultural bond is stronger. When push comes to shove, your fundamental lack of trust, of comfort, shows through.

Without that trust, there is no way to get to stage 5. Nothing may ever make your Spanish colleague less quirky in personal terms. That may just be the way he is. But if you have met with him face to face many times over the years, if you have gotten to know his family, if you have spent private social time together, if your children have stayed at his house and his at yours—then his personal idiosyncrasies do not call into question the deeper cultural values that you both share. And when there is a problem in Spain, you give him the room he needs to deal with it.

Much of this kind of network building happens gradually and informally over time. But certain formal things can help it along. It is important, for example, that no one talks of "domestic" or "home-country" or "overseas" operations. It is important that you do not speak of subsidiaries or affiliates or local hires. The language you speak—and the worldview it implies—must be global. You really have to believe, deep down, that people may work "in" different national environments but are not "of" them. What they are "of" is the global corporation. And that affiliation must be supported, in matters large and small, by the personnel decisions and policies carried out at the center. Evaluations, expectations, qualifications, levels of talent—all these must be equivalent in every part of the world. Thinking about personnel must be truly homogeneous. If it is, strangely enough, local operations will enjoy more, not less, autonomy.

If you have confidence in your colleagues, if they all measure up to the same global standard, you do not worry about trying to micromanage what they do. You will let them do what they think makes sense. You trust their judgment. In traditional multinational organizations, being responsive to local conditions often means being unresponsive to headquarters, and vice versa. Because you worry about people going native and about lack of consistency, you try to enforce some relatively inflexible measure of commonality from the center. In a global organization that operates in an amoebalike fashion, you don't worry about such things because you know your colleagues have internalized the common values and standards and expectations. The appearance of outward conformity matters less because you are confident about inward agreement on values and goals and mission.

Developing such agreement is a time-consuming process. At the personal level, it takes endless face-to-face contacts. Organizationally, you can do it by identifying locals who share the culture and values of their colleagues at the center or by sending out people from the center to local operations. Too often, however, this latter approach turns into a kind of ticket-punching activity—give the up-and-comer a quick stint in a foreign operation.

This is a transitional stage because it is all too easy for managers sent out from the center to "run" Japan or Germany or Italy for a couple of years to have their sights set on returning to the center with a better-looking résumé. Their purpose ought to be to identify and nurture a cadre of local nationals who can take things over in the long run. Sooner or later most of these "visitors" will want to return home. Their children will reach their mid or late teens, and it will be time to think about where they should be in school. When that happens, it is important that local nationals be ready to take over. Otherwise, they will be demoted and a new manager will be sent out from the center. This is a recipe for demotivating people and for destroying trust. No global organization can hold together for long when leadership jerks around like a yo-yo.

This is a major part of what makes stage 5 so hard to reach. The up-front, sustained investment in people and management process is big. When times get tough and money gets tight, there is a temptation to cut back on the travel, the meetings, and the transfers needed to build informal linkages and a shared culture. Controllers look at the numbers and shake their heads.

These are tough issues, but the only source of long-term success is people. You are either seriously committed to developing them or you are not. You develop your people in good times and bad, or you continue to wonder why stage 5 always seems to remain out of reach. More than that, it is actively harmful for an organization to approach stage 5 and then back away and then try again, halfheartedly, some time in the future.

When the long-term network-building process aborts, when it is not really credible, what happens? Some local managers says, Okay, I'm the head of Italy or Germany or Japan. The rest of you do not have a clue about the situation here. You don't understand a thing about it. Look at the numbers. My track record is pretty darn good. So get off my back and let me handle things here my own way, or find someone else to do it. I'm sick and tired of you characters at headquarters trying to second-guess what I do. The choice is simple: Shut up or fire me. This happens often. No one else knows enough to come in and help. Headquarters is not eager to start over from scratch—until, that is, things get so bad it feels it has to make a move. There is no shared conversation, no meeting of the minds. There is only an armed truce.

Even if the person is brilliant, what happens if he gets run over by a truck or decides he wants to go do something else? Or what if the situation changes, and he is no longer the right man for the times? The first Japanese shogun, who founded the Tokugawa shogunate, recognized that the man who conquers the world from horseback is rarely the one who can lead society during a time of peace. He himself was an exception, perhaps the only one in Japan's modern history. He was a master of both the martial and the social arts—the exception that proves the rule. Managers who excel during periods of rapid growth may not be suited to slower-growing, mature businesses.

It is risky, then, to leave things in the hands of so dominant a local king, someone emphatically not part of collegial global network. At best, it is an inflexible arrangement. It is certainly unstable. This is not a good state of affairs, but neither is having headquarters send in a colonial army of occupation. Either way, it is easy to see how things can come apart. Betting so completely on one individual is risky. He might turn out to be the right person. But the odds are against it.

Tearing Down the Pyramid

Amoebalike organizations do not allow such kings to emerge at the top of local pyramids. There will always be strong-willed local leaders—no one wants ineffective people in leadership positions. But there will be no pyramids for them to sit atop. The route to local leadership in global organizations is through active participation in the collegial network of shared values. And when such a network exists, when multiple communication channels develop to put all members in touch with each other, pyramids cannot survive or be built afresh. This is true as long as critical information does not flow down authoritatively from a source on high but, rather, flows in all directions.

Even globally minded corporations still get this wrong. In 1988, for the first time, the German operation of a leading global manufacturer of industrial products sent a team of experts to visit their counterparts in Japan. Why? For the first time the German company was being beaten badly by Japanese competitors in its home markets. For years the German managers had largely ignored their Japanese colleagues. What can they tell us that we don't already know? they wondered. Our share of the market is 70 percent; theirs is only 20 percent. What can they teach us? It turned out, of course, that what their colleagues had learned from twenty hard years of firsthand experience was how to beat the Japanese at their own game. Headquarters never syndicated the information. Even if it had, no one would have paid attention. The company operated around the world; its networks did not.

A major Japanese high-technology firm moved aggressively into Europe and the United States. Its chief executive, the architect of the push into global markets, hired a first-class American to get the United States operations up and running and gave him an up-and-coming star in Japan, who was tagged as the future president of the whole corporation, as his second-in-command. He reports to you, was the CEO's message. Ignore headquarters. Do what you think is best. Take what resources you need. But Americanize our operations. Make us insiders. And that is just what he tried to do. He did ignore headquarters. He did build a system that was culturally out of synch with the rest of the company. And the corporate staff back home undermined him. They withheld support and, in effect, sabotaged his efforts.

Managing networks is an inherently messy and inefficient process. But networks are what hold together an organization based neither on country allegiances nor individual personality but on shared values. It can look sloppy or chaotic. But it is the only way to get over the hurdle to stage 5—and to do so in a manner that is genuinely lasting and sustainable. Many companies have tried to force march their way to globalization by submitting to the dictates of a single dominant leader. But when that leader departs or when the environment shifts, things slip back. Leaders on horseback cannot globalize an organization. Only people linked horizontally in a network can do that.

7

Planting for a Global Harvest

In the garden outside my home in Japan, I grow my favorite mix of plants and flowers—that is, given the kind of soil I have, the exposure, the light, the extremes of temperature. I do what the environment allows and encourages. I get lots of advice, of course, but no green-thumbed expert has yet tried to convince me to lay out a bed for flora indigenous to desert, arctic tundra, or tropical rain forest. They would not grow in Tokyo, and no one would expect them to.

This is plain common sense. Why, then, when managers prepare the ground for the global organizations they hope to grow, do they often pay little attention to the quality of soil, light, temperature, and exposure? Why do they talk and plan—and commit time and resources—as if one special plant could grow equally well in all possible climates and situations?

The question of the fit between an organization and its environment is not new; nor has it become important in the context of recent corporate efforts to operate in a genuinely global fashion. But the movement toward globalization has given it a new urgency and raised the penalty for getting the answer wrong.

As a Garden

When globalization efforts fail, chances are it's because of a mistaken vision of the organization—and the values—needed for success. During the past few years, I have received many inquiries from CEOs in Europe and the United States who want to set up operations in the other part of the Triad—Japan. Japan, they tell me, is the future, and their companies need to be a part of it. Yes, they have waited longer than they should have, but now they want in and they want in quickly. Could I help?

My first response is to press them for the strategic thinking underlying their urgent wish to enter Japan. Do the markets make sense for them? Do their products appeal to local tastes? Are there local players with whom they can link up? In most cases, the CEOs have done their homework pretty well. They have good answers to my questions.

Then I ask how many of the, say, 60,000 people in their companies speak Japanese. Silence. I ask again. Well, none. Next I ask how many of their people have really studied the day-to-day management issues of running a business in Japan. Once more, silence. After that I ask them to write down the names of all the Japanese businesspeople they personally know well enough to spend a social weekend with. More silence. Then I suggest that perhaps they need to rethink their expectations about timing.

Tell me about your company's history, I say. When was it founded? How long did it take you and your predecessors to build it into a dominant force in your home country? No silence now; we're on familiar ground. Why, it took us fifty years, they tell me, to go from a tiny, midwestern manufacturer to a major electronics producer. And only in the last fifteen years or so have we begun to move into Europe.

Fifty years, I'd repeat back to them, to get where you are in the United States. And fifteen years to explore the ground in Europe. So why do you expect to be able to get things up and running in Japan in anything less than ten or fifteen years? Japan is now roughly half the size of the American market. It is one of the toughest markets in the world. Why then shouldn't it take you more than twenty-five years to develop a position here comparable to the one you have built at home?

The expectation, of course, is that getting true religion means you ought to be able to suspend the calendar. Well, things do not work that way. The planning horizon at most companies is, at best, five years. So is the average tenure of CEOs. However, those who have only recently set their sights on Japan often talk as if their products should be able to land one week and meet with headline-making success the next. All they need is to link up with a good advertising agency, a good consulting firm, a good team of lawyers.

But what about the people to make all this work? Who is going to run things in Japan? No problem, they tell me. We'll use headhunters. But things do not work that way either.

When I explain these things, most CEOs seem disappointed. They even say that what I'm describing is another form of Japanese nontariff barrier. One even told me, "Look, we know a congressman from the state where we have our headquarters. He is a pretty hawkish protectionist. Do you think it would help any if we got him to put some pressure on Japan?" "Look," I told him. "That's not the conversation that matters. In an age when business success depends on staying close to customers, my experience—without exception—has been that successful companies spend time in conversation, in close touch, with what is going on in the marketplace. Unsuccessful companies run to Washington or Brussels or Kasumizaseki [the district in Tokyo where all the Japanese governmental agencies are located]."

The primary reason hurried efforts fail, the reason it takes so long to establish a global presence in Japan (or in any large market), the reason that checkbook-driven shortcuts do not work, is people—and the *values* they do or do not carry with them. Even if headhunters find you local managers who can walk on water, they cannot know your organization, cannot know how it operates, cannot know the other managers in the network, at least not overnight. Nor can they share the values that hold your organization together—at a time when it is precisely those values that *do* hold your organization together. This is no reflection on their credentials or ability or promise. They simply have not had the time to learn, to internalize the culture of your organization.

Soil, Tree, Fruits

The cultural environment in which managers work has several different, though related, dimensions. So far I have been talking about it in its broadest, most inclusive sense: the set of universally shared values that holds together the members of a genuinely amoebalike, network-based, stage 5 global organization.

When a company is small, or operates in a single location, these values can remain implicit and informal. There is merit in trying to make them explicit, but the penalty for not doing so is relatively light. If your colleagues work just down the hall and you see them daily, a large amount of communication takes place in the normal course of events. You sit together at lunch. You bump into each other in the hallway. But as soon as your company has multiple locations, an important part of the communication flow gets lost. What once happened naturally now has to be planned.

You have to work much harder, of course, if your colleagues are not in a second location across town but in another city or another country. The importance of making shared values explicit, of actively working at them, grows as distance and diversity increase. Not only are the channels of communication tougher to maintain; the variation in your experiences and in the business environments with which you have to deal increases as well. Assumptions that made sense in a local market with a finite set of customers may not apply so well when you and your colleagues are operating in different countries.

As companies become global, both problems take on even greater dimensions. First the time and effort required to learn and maintain the organization's culture reach a whole new order of magnitude. And second, the local aspects of the shared values that once held things together now work to drive them apart. Consequently, if these values are to stay meaningful, they must be made explicit and they must be purged of their provincialism. In other words, there has to be a coherent, nationalityless mission statement in which the values can take root.

But this is only part of the challenge. Day to day, you and your colleagues must wrestle, as well, with the particular industry setting in which you operate. In this sense, I have come to think that the culture of an organization is like the soil; a business is like a tree growing in the soil; and profits are like the fruits of the tree. An effective corporation will have the same kind of soil, with the same pH, in all the regions of the world where it operates. And in that soil will grow similar kinds of trees. If you put the wrong seeds in this or that patch of ground, if you try to grow someone else's kind of tree, if you play the mergers and acquisitions game and just want to steal the fruits without planting or fertilizing anything—that is, if you do not take the time to grow healthy trees in the spots suitable for them—you will never be able to reap a proper long-term harvest.

Few, if any, companies have been able to force radically different kinds of trees to root strongly and grow well in precisely the same soil. If you want to harvest a variety of fruits, then you have to plant each tree in its appropriate setting. You need a healthy environment, with the right leadership style, accounting and planning systems, evaluation and reward systems, and so on. For global companies, this means looking at industry-specific organizational issues in a new way.

Once your business horizons are no longer constrained by national borders, you will probably find that many of the things that made you a first-rate competitor at home will not apply elsewhere—at least, not in quite the same way. The local infrastructure may well be different; likewise, the nature and extent of government influence, the tax codes, the expectations of customers, and so on. Each national market has its own rules for determining success and failure, and there is no guarantee that those rules will be the ones you know best.

In Japan, for example, one very popular new product is an electronically controlled, heated toilet seat with a built-in bidet. For the Japanese people, it is an appealing home appliance that is sold through each manufacturer's company shops. You walk in and make your selection. In the United States and Europe, however, it is not so simple. There are unions to be dealt with, and the unions that handle electrical appliances do not do plumbing work. Thus only part of the skills and know-how that make Japanese producers successful at home can be transferred to these other environments. To succeed there, other competencies are needed. The relevant industry-specific business culture cannot be transplanted lock, stock, and barrel.

Or think about the antitrust environment in the United States, especially in the pre-Reagan days. If competitors talked to each other the way they regularly and legally do in Japan, they would get to relax and read their next annual reports in a federal penitentiary. For Japanese managers coming to the United States, much about the general business environment is radically different from what they know at home. Worrying about building good products is not enough. They also have to worry about getting sued, about what the Occupational Health and Safety Administration might say, about how well they meet the provisions of the Equal Employment Opportunities Act, about what the Federal Trade Commission is up to, about what they say in their internal memos, about the latest preoccupation of the hordes of lawyers who swarm relentlessly from courtroom to courtroom. In Japan they usually don't have to worry about any of this. They can focus on meeting customer needs and on developing products with impact, not on checking every thought that pops into their heads with a cast of thousands. Knowing their business is enough. This is what makes competition so difficult in Japan. To operate in the United States they have to learn a whole new business culture.

They also have to learn the salient characteristics of the new markets they want to serve. Advertising, for example, matters much less in developing countries than it does in the industrialized world. In the NIEs, only those companies that have received government licenses can serve particular markets. This limits competition and changes the nature of the game. There is no need to drum up demand because supply has been artificially constrained. The sophistication of the market is different, and so are the rules.

There is a third dimension to culture as well. Global companies must be concerned with universal values and with the variation in national environments in each of their businesses. They must also pay attention to the variety of businesses they attempt to manage under a single organizational roof. No longer is the key question how to combine these disparate business units into divisions or sectors based solely on assumed similarities among customers or markets. The more important question is how to combine them into coherent culture units that provide a common soil in which each business can flourish.

Think, for a moment, of a company that builds such things as ships or aircraft or power-generation plants. Imagine that it is absolutely first class in making large industrial systems to order. More than likely, it has tried to diversify into different product lines, perhaps computers and air conditioners. Equally likely, it has always failed. How can it be, you wonder, that a company can do so well in industries as complex and varied as aircraft and power-generation equipment but can't make a go of such mass-produced items as office equipment? It does not make sense.

It does. When you build planes or ships or power plants, your R&D looks ten or twenty years into the future. You get to see your customers, talk to them in detail, find out exactly what they want and when they want it. You make everything to order. You do not have to guess what customer preferences will be in a year or two or the level of demand for your products next month or the month after that. Customers tell you. Once they have spoken and you have signed the contract for a delivery date three to five years down the road, you can set to work making money by finding ways to cut manufacturing costs. In longer-term businesses like these, where manufacturing costs account for roughly 90 percent of total costs, cost reduction is the shortest route to profit.

When it comes to air conditioners, everything changes. The sense of timing is different. The accounting and planning systems are different. The cost focus is different. Mass production in the face of slippery market forecasts and unknown customers becomes the focusing task. The planning horizon is, at best, one year. Nothing is made to order, and manufacturing represents perhaps 30 percent of total costs. You take your best guess, imagine what your hypothetical customers will want in a year or so, and jump in. If the summer is cold and wet, all your best plans count for nothing. If it proves unusually hot, there is no way you can catch up with demand. You never really get to know your customers. Instead, you make commitments based on abstract numbers for an abstract marketplace. Continually playing the "perfect" game, based on a gamble you take twice a year, is the key to business success.

It should be no surprise that the accounting systems and organizational structures best suited to aircraft or ship production provide infertile ground for managers trying to build an air conditioner or personal computer business. It is not possible to grow both of them successfully in the same soil. They belong to different culture units.

When, however, the ground is hospitable to air conditioners and other white goods, managers know about distribution channels for consumer goods. An experienced sales force is in place. The planning horizon is six months. The company is geared for white goods. In fact, with even a marginal product, it can capture 30 percent market share and earn attractive returns if it has a perfect infrastructure in place. If, however, the same company were to try its hand at computers or communications equipment, it would fail as badly as the builder of ships and aircraft did with air conditioners. The time horizons, revenue and cost relationships, and management systems—the soil—would be different.

The concept that software is more important than hardware would be difficult for the company to accept. The idea that their product was a communications network—not a discrete piece of hardware—would be alien.

A growing number of research institutes want to be consultants that serve clients in the same way my management consulting firm does. When a research institute does its work properly, it comes up with a set of findings that are accurate and precise. Today the weather forecast is for clear skies with a 20 percent chance of rain. If the institute is right in its findings, consistently so, then it succeeds. Management consultants ultimately do not care about such things. For us, such a prediction is just one of many factors that we need to take into consideration. When we do our work properly, what we say to a CEO is, Do not take your umbrella today; you will not need it. We provide assistance for a CEO's judgment—fact-based, of course, but a judgment nonetheless. Or we say, You must take your umbrella today, or you will be miserable. We need to understand the forecast of a 20 percent chance of rain. We need to have a point of view about its accuracy. Maybe the real number is closer to 40 percent. If so, would our advice be any different? The facts are where we begin. Our work is to digest them and then say take the umbrella or leave it.

Research institutes and consultancies are very different cultural environments. Some of the same analytical skills are relevant to both, but the expert who is most comfortable deciding whether the 20 percent figure is off by some fraction is not going to be comfortable telling CEOs what to do with rain gear. Nor can the organizations in which both sorts of work get done be run the same way.

Too often, managers fail to pay attention to the natural boundaries of these culture units (as opposed to industry sector–based units). This is especially true with efforts to diversify out of familiar business lines. Many such efforts miscarry because the people making the decisions are those who grew up in the original culture. They ignore the differences in soil that make it possible for different businesses to grow. In effect, they want to sit in their offices, prop their feet on their desks, and look out their windows at all their corporate activities without once turning their heads or adjusting their gaze. They want to use common systems, common yardsticks, and common assumptions across their wide range of businesses and across the entire globe. They want to compare things easily using precisely the same yardsticks from product line to product line. They want simplicity. What they get is chaos.

Culture units matter. Most large companies got large by building dominant positions in what turned out to be huge markets, not by mastering the ins and outs of a wide range of businesses. Think how many leading global companies are largely monocultural, in my sense of the term. General Motors is 88 percent automobiles; Royal Dutch/Shell, 88 percent petroleum; Exxon, 87 percent petroleum; Ford, 93 percent automobiles. Much the same is true of IBM, Toyota, British Petroleum, Mobil, and many other large and powerful companies.

General Electric (GE) is in a wide variety of businesses. But inspection shows that many of its activities—heavy electrical products and aircraft engines, for example—readily fall into the same culture units. Kidder Peabody is another story. It can flourish under the GE umbrella, but not if its cultural identity, its particular soil, goes untended. It needs to be managed in an entirely different way: as a separate culture unit, with its own accounting system, planning horizon, style, and staff.

It is possible, of course, to find some common denominators that run across a series of cultural units—IBM's focus on providing solutions for customers, for example, or Johnson and Johnson's sustained attention to the needs of hospitals and nurses. Where they work, however, these common denominators usually take the form of the universal values I discussed earlier, the high-level abstractions that hold global organizations together. They do not speak to the practical issue of how best to cultivate individual businesses.

How can you tell one patch of soil from another? What makes

each distinctive? Where in the garden do you draw the line in efforts to nurture and support different culture units? Coming up with a good soil analysis takes good answers to such questions as:

1. Is the business primarily a manufacturing activity? What makes up its cost structure? What do end users really pay a price for?
2. Is the key product made in large numbers, many varieties, small lots?
3. What is the pattern of investment? Metal smelting, for example, requires large-scale but infrequent investment; home appliances take many small infusions of capital.
4. What is the time horizon of the business? Does the business make a return on its investment in ten years or five? Or does it, like branded goods, earn a return in two to three years—if it earns one at all?
5. What is the life of the product? With polyvinyl chloride, which has a long life, you can play with supply and demand and target long-term changes in the industry's cost curve. With office products, which typically last five years or so, you can both plan and harvest long term. With cameras and other consumer electronics, product life is short, and your strategies must take that into account.

These forces—fundamental economics, type of production, investment patterns, time horizon, and product life—influence what middle managers do more deeply than anything their bosses tell them directly. If they are stubborn or insubordinate, it is because these forces shape the systems and the assumptions in which all managers operate; they define the culture, and the culture determines what will and will not grow.

Most successful global corporations run things not from a single, central point of control but through a network of regional organizations that keeps managers close to key markets and customers. As I've noted, this approach works only when the strong pull of local interests and concerns can be offset by an equally strong set of values that all these managers share. Making this creative tension work is an important part of the CEO's role. Other managers, even those high up, have to be steeped in—and committed to—the cultures of the individual businesses or groups of businesses for which they are responsible. CEOs have a different task. Their job is to see that each culture unit is kept separate and distinct and is managed in the fashion most appropriate to its special environment. Their primary responsibility, then, is to make certain that no "spillover" occurs from one of those units to another, no unintended leakage of culture-specific systems or approaches. It is also to make sure that the firm's monocultural control staff does not impose its own rigid, one-size-fits-all mentality on any of those units. Some basic values and approaches do need to be shared. Otherwise, however, it is the CEO's job to protect against the homogenization of culture units.

These shared values are an important part of the cultural environment, the soil, in which any global company tries to root its far-flung activities. On a business-by-business basis, however, that soil has other important ingredients—in particular, the characteristics just noted, which have much to say about what kinds of endeavor will flourish in this or that garden plot. Shared values are not at odds with these variations in soil. They hold together managers' efforts to take variations seriously and match them with the culture units to which they are best suited.

Planting for a global harvest, then, is a painstaking, iterative process of balancing local needs with shared values and balancing particular growing conditions with the requirements of each crop. It is work that takes determination and a steady hand. Longer term, you have to build a separate global business for each of your culture units. Commonalities in a business culture are so important to economic success that they easily outweigh traditional differences in language or secular culture.

This is particularly true in sophisticated markets. Often, in a developing economy, you find that one company dominates the market in a wide variety of businesses—Thailand's Siam Cement, for example, or Korea's five *zaibatsu* groups or pre–World War II Japan's Mitsuis and Sumitomos. When you look more closely, however, you see that the great strength of these companies usually lies in their influence on the public decision-making process (licenses for production, for example). They also benefit from being able to acquire and train good people and from being able to borrow technology and know-how from abroad. When the market becomes more demanding, however, success depends much more heavily on how well you have been able to adjust your business to local soil conditions. Gardening is an activity that must be done up close.

8

The Global Logic of Strategic Alliances

Corporate leaders are beginning to learn what the leaders of nations have always known: In a complex, uncertain world filled with dangerous opponents, it is best not to go it alone. Great powers operating across broad theaters of engagement have made common cause with others whose interests ran parallel with their own. There is no shame in this. Entente—the striking of an alliance—is a responsible part of every good strategist's repertoire.

But managers have been slow to experiment with genuinely strategic alliances. They have tried joint ventures and long-term contractual relationships, certainly, but rarely attempted the forging of entente. A real alliance compromises the fundamental independence of economic actors, and managers don't like that. For them, management has come to mean total control. Alliances mean sharing control. The one precludes the other.

In stable competitive environments, this allergy to loss of control exacts little penalty. But this is not the case in a changeable world of rapidly globalizing markets and industries—a world of converging consumer tastes, rapidly spreading technology, escalating fixed costs, and growing protectionism. Globalization mandates alliances, makes them absolutely essential to strategy.

Why, then, the reluctance of so many companies either to experiment with alliances or to stick with them long enough to learn how to make them work? To some extent, both foot dragging and early exit are born of fear—fear that the alliance will turn out to be a Trojan horse that affords potential competitors easy access to home markets. But there is also an impression that alliances represent, at best, a convenience, a quick-and-dirty means of entry into foreign markets. These attitudes make managers skittish and impatient.

Unless you understand the long-run strategic value of entente, you will grow frustrated when it proves—as it must—not to be a cheap and easy way of responding to the uncertainties of globalization. If you expect more of your partners than is reasonable, you will blame them too quickly when things do not go as planned. Chances are your impatience will make you much less tolerant of them than you would be of your own subsidiary overseas.

When you expect convenience, you rarely have much patience for the demanding work of building a strong competitive position. Nor do you remember all the up-front overseas investments that you did *not* have to make. And without memory or patience, you risk precipitating exactly what you fear most: an unhappy or unsatisfied partner that decides to bow out of the alliance and try to tackle your markets on its own.

Glaxo, a British pharmaceutical company, for example, did not want to establish a full business system in each country where it did business. Especially given its costly commitment to top-flight R&D, it did not see how it could—or why it should—build an extensive sales and service network to cover all the hospitals in Japan and the United States. So it decided to link up with first-class partners in Japan, swap its best drugs with each of them, and focus its own resources on generating greater sales from its established network in Europe. *That* kind of value creation and delivery is what alliances make possible.

What does this mean? If you don't have to invest in your own overseas sales force, don't do it. If you run a pharmaceutical company with a good drug to distribute in Japan, but no sales force to do it, find someone in Japan who also has a good product but no sales force in your country. You get double the profit by putting two strong drugs through your fixed-cost sales network, and so does your new ally. Why duplicate such huge expenses all down the line? Why go head-to-head? Why not join forces to maximize contribution to each other's fixed costs?

Maximizing the contribution to fixed costs does not come naturally. Tradition and pride make companies want to be the best at everything, to do everything themselves. But companies can no longer afford this solitary stance. Take the machine-tool market. If a German manufacturer clearly excels in custom-made segments, why should such highly automated Japanese producers as Mori Seiki and Yamazaki tackle those segments too? Why not tie up with the Germans and let them dominate those segments worldwide? Why not try to supply them with certain common components that you can make better—or more cheaply—than they do? Why not disaggregate the product and the business system and put together an alliance that delivers the most value to customers while making the greatest contribution to both partners' fixed costs?

Why not do this? Companyism gets in the way. So does a competitor-focused approach to strategy. And so does not knowing what it takes to operate globally and how alliances help with fixed costs.

Dangers of Equity

Global alliances are not the only valid mechanisms for boosting contribution to fixed costs. A strong brand umbrella can always cover additional products. You can always give heightened attention to, say, an expensive distribution system that you have already built in Japan or Europe. And there is always the possibility of buying a foreign company.

With enough time, money, and luck you can expand brands and build up distribution yourself—you can do everything yourself. But all three are in short supply. In particular, you do not have the time to establish new markets one by one throughout the Triad. The "cascade" model of expansion no longer works. Today you have to be in all important markets simultaneously if you are going to keep competitors from establishing their positions. Globalization will not wait. You need alliances and you need them now. But not the traditional kind.

In the past, companies commonly approached international expansion by doing it on their own, acquiring others, or establishing joint ventures. The latter two approaches carry important equity-related concerns. Let equity—the classic instrument of capitalism—into the picture, and you start to worry about control and return on investment. There is pressure to get money back fast for the money you put in and dividends from the paper you hold.

It's a reflex. The analysts expect it of you. So do the business press, colleagues, and stockholders. They'll nod politely when you talk about improved sales or long-term strategic benefits. But what everybody really wants fast is chart-topping ROI.

Managers must also overcome the misconception that total control increases chances of success. Things can quickly go sour in companies that have enjoyed successful joint ventures for years when they move to a literal, equity-, and contract-based mode of ownership. The details vary with the particular case, but the slide into disarray and disappointment usually starts with the typical arguments that broke up one transnational chemical joint venture:

(Soon to be) New Owner: You guys never make decisions in time.

(Soon to be) Former Partner: Speedy decisions are not everything. Consensus is more important.

NO: Well, just tell the dealers that our products are the best in the world. Tell them that they sell everywhere, except here.

FP: But the dealers complain that your products are just okay, not great. Even worse, they are not really tailored to the needs or aesthetic preferences of local customers.

NO: Nonsense. What customers buy, everywhere in the world, is the physical performance of the product. No one matches us in performance.

FP: Perhaps. Still, the dealers report that your products are not neatly packaged and often have scratches on the surface.

NO: But that has no effect on performance.

FP: Tell that to the dealers. They say they cannot readily see— or sell—the performance difference you're talking about so they have to fall back on aesthetics, where your products are weak. We'll have to reduce price.

NO: Don't you dare. We succeeded in the United States and in Europe by keeping our prices at least 5 percent above those of our competitors. If we're having trouble in Japan it's because of you. Your obvious lack of effort, knowledge, even confidence in our products—that's what keeps them from selling. Besides, your parent keeps on sending our joint venture group a bunch of bumbling old incompetents for managers. We rarely get the good people. Maybe the idea is to kill off our relationship entirely so they can start up a unit of their own making imitation products.

FP: Well, if you feel that way, there is not much point in our continuing on together.

NO: Glad you said that. We'll buy up the other 50 percent of the equity and go it on our own.

FP: Good luck. By the way, how many Japanese-speaking managers do you have in your company—that is, after we pull out all the "bumbling old incompetents" from our joint venture?

NO: None. But don't worry. We'll just hire a bunch of head-hunters and get started up in record time.

Back when this arrangement was a functioning joint venture, both partners—and especially the middle managers—made an effort to have things work. Under a cloud of 100 percent control, things are different. You can buy a company's equity, but you cannot buy the mind or the spirit or the initiative or the devotion of its people. Nor can you just go hire replacements. In different environments, the availability of key professional services— managerial, legal, and so on—varies considerably.

The lesson is that having control does not necessarily mean a better-managed company. You cannot manage a global company through control. In fact, control is the last resort. It's what you fall back on when everything else fails and when you're willing to risk demoralizing workers and managers.

This need for control is deeply rooted. The tradition of Western capitalism lies behind it, a tradition that has taught managers the incorrect arithmetic that equates 51 percent with 100 percent and 49 percent with 0 percent. Fifty-one percent buys you full legal control. But it is control of activities in a foreign market, about which you may know little as you sit removed from the needs of customers in your offices in Manhattan, Tokyo, or Frankfurt.

When Americans and Europeans come to Japan, they all want 51 percent. That's the magic number because it ensures majority position and control over personnel, brand decisions, and invest- ment choices. But good partnerships, like good marriages, don't work on the basis of ownership or control. It takes effort and commitment and enthusiasm from both sides if either is to realize the hoped-for benefits. You cannot own a successful partner any more than you can own a husband or a wife.

In time, as the relationship between partners deepens and as mutual trust and confidence build, there may come a point when it no longer makes sense to remain two separate entities. Strategy, values, and culture might all match up so well that both sides want to finish the work of combination. Hewlett-Packard's pres- ence in Japan started out in 1963, for example, as a 51–49 joint venture with Yokogawa Electric. Over two decades, enough con- fidence had built up that in 1983, Yokogawa Electric gave Hewl- ett-Packard another 24 percent.

Thus it took two decades for Hewlett-Packard to reach a significant ownership position. Control was never the objective. All along the objective was to do things right and serve customers well by learning how to operate as a genuine insider in Japan. As a result, Hewlett-Packard now owns 75 percent of a $750 million company in Japan that earns 6.6 percent net profit after tax.

An emphasis on control through equity, however, immediately poisons the relationship. Instead of focusing on contribution to fixed costs, one company imperialistically tells the other, "Look, I've got a big equity stake in you. You don't give me all the dividends I want, so get busy and distribute my product. I'm not going to distribute yours, though. Remember, you work for me."

This kind of attitude problem prevents the development of intercompany management skills, which are critical for success in today's global environment. Peter L. Bonfield, chairman and managing director of International Computers Ltd. (ICL), distributes plastic name-card holders to all his people who are in touch with Fujitsu, ICL's mainframe computer partner in Japan. On one side there is a place for the cards; on the other, a proven list of "Do's" for making such collaborative arrangements work. There is nothing here about 51 percent or establishing control.

Equity by itself is not the problem in building successful alliances. In Japan there are a lot of "group companies" known as *keiretsu,* where an equity stake of, say, 3 percent to 5 percent keeps both partners interested in each other's welfare without threatening either's autonomy. Stopping that far short of a controlling position keeps the equity holder from treating the other company as if it were a subsidiary. Small equity investments like these may be the way to go.

Parental Consent

Joint ventures can work, but there are two obstacles that can trip them up. First, there is a contract, and contracts—even at their best—can reflect an understanding of costs and markets and tech-

ICL's "Do's" for Successful Collaboration

1. Treat the collaboration as a personal commitment. It's people that make partnerships work.

2. Anticipate that it will take up management time. If you can't spare the time, don't start it.

3. Mutual respect and trust are essential. If you don't trust the people you are negotiating with, forget it.

4. Remember that both partners must get something out of it (money, eventually). Mutual benefit is vital. This will probably mean you've got to give something up. Recognize this from the outset.

5. Make sure you tie up a tight legal contract. Don't put off resolving unpleasant or contentious issues until "later." However, once signed, the contract should be put away. If you refer to it, something is wrong with the relationship.

6. Recognize that during the course of a collaboration, circumstances and markets change. Recognize your partner's problems and be flexible.

7. Make sure you and your partner have mutual expectations of the collaboration and its time scale. One happy and one unhappy partner is a formula for failure.

8. Get to know your opposite numbers at all levels socially. Friends take longer to fall out.

9. Appreciate that cultures—both geographic and corporate—are different. Don't expect a partner to act or respond identically to you. Find out the true reason for a particular response.

10. Recognize your partner's interests and independence.

11. Even if the arrangement is tactical in your eyes, make sure you have corporate approval. Your tactical activity may be a key piece in an overall strategic jigsaw puzzle. With corporate commitment to the partnership, you can act with the positive authority needed in these relationships.

12. Celebrate achievement together. It's a shared elation, and you'll have earned it!

Postscript
Two further things to bear in mind:

1. If you're negotiating a product deal with an original equipment manufacturer look for a quid pro quo. Remember that another product may offer more in return.
2. Joint development agreements must include joint marketing arrangements. You need the largest market possible to recover development costs and to get volume/margin benefits.

nologies only at the moment companies sign them. When things change, the partners don't really try to compromise and adjust. They look to the contract and start pointing fingers. They go easy on their own companies and tolerate their own mistakes. Tolerance goes way down when partners cause mistakes.

The second problem with joint ventures is that parent companies behave as parents everywhere do. They don't give their children the breathing space—or the time—they need to grow. Nor do they react kindly when their children want to expand, especially if it's into areas the parents want to keep for themselves. "Keep your hands off" is the message they send; not a good way to motivate anyone.

Fuji-Xerox, for example, a very successful 50–50 arrangement between Rank-Xerox and Fuji Film, earns high profits on its $3 billion annual sales and attracts some of the best people in Japan to work for it. Equally important, it has enough autonomy to get actively involved in such new areas as digital imaging technology, even though both parents have strong interests there themselves. The head of Fuji-Xerox, Yotaro Kobayashi, who is the son of the founder of Fuji Film, now sits on the board of Xerox, which has benefited greatly from Fuji-Xerox's experience in battling the Japanese companies that have attacked Xerox's position in the mid-range to low-end copier segments in the United States.

Most such arrangements, however, are not so happy. Many

parents are reluctant, for example, to put all the business functions into a joint venture that it would need to be a freestanding entity. Say they keep all of R&D and manufacturing to themselves and provide their joint venture with a charter—and capability—limited to marketing. Sooner or later at least one of the parents is going to decide that what it wants most in the world is to move more boxes. The pressure for volume is on, it admits, and the only thing to do is to get more product out the door. And its expectation, its insistence, is that the venture will help it do just that. Peddling additional boxes might not add value to the venture's customers. It might deflect its managers' attention from more important things—more important to the venture, that is, not to the parents. But as far as the parent is concerned, when necessity calls, the venture is a box-mover.

That is not quite the way the venture's managers see it. If they lack the functional capabilities to define and implement their own strategy, they are forever at the mercy of parental whim. It does not take a genius to see here the potential for major conflicts of interest—not least because parents often conveniently forget their whims when it comes to evaluating the venture's performance. The deal implied in the order for the venture to move more boxes—do this for us now and when evaluation time comes, we will adjust our expectations accordingly—turns out to be no deal at all.

The potential for conflict is not random but systemic. Say a parent wants its venture to sell more boxes in Japan. Fair enough, the managers respond, but that means we will need to jack up our advertising budget from $2.5 million to $5 million. No way, comes the response. You ought to be able to do it just by working harder and smarter with the resources you've got. That's what we pay you for, anyway. And if you can't or won't do it, we will find someone who can. Meanwhile, when the year end comes around, the parent is going to want to make its balance sheet look as healthy as possible by getting inventory off its books and onto the venture's books. No one is fooled by this kind of legerdemain, but no one is immune to it either. The magic translation of excess boxes into sales for the parent and unwanted inventory for the venture may have become an annual rite, but it is one that tends to be forgotten when performance gets reviewed. Outside analysts, not parents, worry about quality of earnings.

Sometimes the conflicts are even more direct. Imagine a parent in the financial services industry with a venture that provides fee-based investment advice. If the parent makes its money from transactions of one sort or another—equity sales, for example—not even a boy scout will believe that the venture will escape pressure, implicit or explicit, to push the parent's stocks and to pay its commissions. Or think of a construction company's interior design venture. If the venture is any good, it will want to sell its services to firms that compete with its parent, and the parent will want to use its services even when the property in question does not really call for them. Worse, think of a construction or property management and repair firm with a venture that does building maintenance. The parent wants to convince owners to carry out costly repairs; the venture wants to maintain the property so well that such repairs are not needed.

Now, these conflicts would also be a problem if the relationship were that of a parent to a subsidiary or to an alliance-based affiliate and not to a joint venture. With a venture, however, they are usually more troublesome, because ventures are less likely to have a full range of functional capabilities—that is, are less likely to be freestanding entities. The practical effect of such incompleteness is to skew expectations improperly. When ventures cannot assert their independence because they lack the means, even the best intentioned of parents will push harder than they should.

This is not to say that it is a good thing for ventures or subsidiaries or affiliates to act against the interests of their parents. The basic purpose of intelligent corporate relationship design is to create arrangements that allow the interests of each party to complement those of the other. It is merely a reminder that providing value to customers and maximizing contribution to fixed costs is, at best, a difficult balancing act. When there can be effective pressure from one side only, the odds increase that the balance finally achieved will be one-sided and unstable.

Examples like that of Fuji-Xerox show, however, that it is possible to strike a healthy balance, even in joint venture arrangements. When each party understands the other's mission, when goals are sufficiently explicit and formal that suspicion of motives is not permitted to take root, when the best people with proven track records take up leadership roles in the venture so that no one can doubt their competence or their credibility, when informal channels of communication are kept open and are used regularly, and when parents are able to keep their hands off but remain close enough to be able to jump in knowledgeably when help is needed—in such conditions, ventures can flourish. It is possible to keep both parties from being so afraid of potential conflicts that nothing happens and, at the same time, to give the venture enough confidence that it can pursue its own ends. There does not have to be either bloodshed or paralysis. There can be an effective balance.

A Marriage of Equals

In general, however, most parents are not so tolerant of their joint ventures' own ambitions. All too often there is either bloodshed or paralysis. Are there better ways to go global than a regular sacrifice of the firstborn? Yes.

Going global is what parents should do together—through alliances that address the issue of fixed costs. Nissan distributes Volkswagens in Japan; Volkswagen sells Nissan's four-wheel-drive cars in Europe. Mazda and Ford swap cars in the Triad; GM and Toyota both collaborate and compete in the United States and Australia. Continental Tyre, General Tire (now owned by Continental), Yokohama Rubber, and Toyo Tire share R&D and swap production. In the United States, for example, General Tire supplies several Japanese transplants on behalf of Yokohama and

Toyo, both of which supply tires on behalf of General and Continental to car companies in Japan. No equity changes hands.

In the pharmaceutical industry, where both ends of the business system (R&D and distribution) represent unusually high fixed costs, companies regularly allow their strong products to be distributed by (potential) competitors with excellent distribution systems in key foreign markets. In the United States, Marion Laboratories distributes Tanabe's Herbesser and Chugai's Ulcerim; Merck, Yamanouchi's Gaster; Eli Lilly, Fujisawa's Cefamezin. In Japan, Shionogi distribures Lilly's Ceclor as Kefral (1988 sales: $700 million). Sankyo distributes Squibb's Capoten; Takeda, Bayer's Adalat; Fujisawa, SmithKline's Tagamet. Sales in Japan of each of these medicines in 1989 were on the order of $300 million.

The distribution of drugs is a labor- and relationship-intensive process. It takes a force of more than one thousand detail people to have any real effect on Japanese medicine. Thus, unless you are committed to building and sustaining such a fixed cost in Japan, it makes sense to collaborate with someone who has such a force already in place—and who can reciprocate elsewhere in the Triad.

Despite the typical "United States vs. Japan" political rhetoric, the semiconductor industry has given rise to many forms of alliances. Most companies feel shorthanded in their R&D, so they swap licenses aggressively. Different forces prompted cooperative arrangements in the nuclear industry. General Electric, Toshiba, Hitachi, ASEA, AMU, and KWU (Siemens) banded together during the late 1970s to develop an improved nuclear boiling water reactor. They shared their upstream R&D on a global basis but kept downstream construction and local customer relationships to themselves. During the 1980s the first three (core) members of the alliance continued their R&D collaboration and, in fact, developed an advanced boiling water reactor concept. This time around, they split the orders from Tokyo Electric Power, among others, one-third each. As confidence builds, the activities open to joint participation can begin to encompass the entire business system.

Hitachi Kenki, a maker of construction equipment, has a loose alliance in hydraulic excavators with Deere & Co. in North America and with Fiat-Allis in Europe. Because Hitachi's product line was too narrow for it to set up its own distribution networks throughout the Triad, it tied up with partners that have strong networks already in place, as well as good additional products of their own, such as bulldozers and wheel-loaders, to fill in the gaps in its product line. So effective have these arrangements been that the partners are now even committed to the joint development of a new wheel-loader.

In the oligopolistic sheet-glass industry, there is a noteworthy alliance between PPG and Asahi Glass, which began in 1966 with a joint venture in Japan to produce polyvinyl chloride. In 1985 the same pair formed a joint automotive glass venture in the United States in hopes of capturing the business of Japanese automakers with American production facilities. They built a second such plant in 1988. That same year they set up a chloride and caustic soda joint venture in Indonesia, along with some local participants and Mitsubishi Trading Company. During all this time, however, they remained fierce global competitors in the sheet-glass business.

Another long-term relationship is the one between Brown Shoe and Nippon Shoe, which introduced a new technology back in 1962 to produce Brown's "Regal" shoes. Today the relationship encompasses several other brands of Brown's shoes. For Brown, this has proven a most effective way to participate in a Japanese market for leather goods that would be otherwise closed to them for both social reasons (historically, Japanese tanners have been granted special privileges) and reasons of appropriate skill (Brown's expertise in, for example, managing its own retail chains is not so relevant in an environment where sky-high real estate prices make direct company ownership of retail shops prohibitively expensive).

There are more examples, but the pattern is obvious: a prudent, non–equity-dependent set of arrangements through which globally active companies can maximize the contribution to their fixed costs. These alliances are an important part of the way companies get back to strategy.

Bad Accounting

One clear change of mind necessary to make alliances work is a shift from a focus on return on investments (ROI) to a focus on return on sales (ROS). An ROS orientation means that managers will concern themselves with the ongoing business benefits of the alliance, not just sit around and wait for a healthy return on their initial investment. Equity investments almost always have an overtone of one company trying to control another with money. But few businesses succeed because of control. Most make it because of motivation, entrepreneurship, customer relationships, creativity, persistence, and attention to the "softer" aspects of organization, such as values and skills.

An alliance is a lot like a marriage. There may be no formal contract. There is no buying and selling of equity. There are few, if any, rigidly binding provisions. It is a loose, evolving kind of relationship. There are guidelines and expectations, but no one expects a precise, measured return on the initial commitment. Both partners bring to an alliance a faith that they will be stronger together than either would be separately. Both believe that each has unique skills and functional abilities the other lacks. And both have to work diligently over time to make the union successful.

When one partner is weak or lazy or won't make an effort to explore what the two can do together, things can come apart. One-sidedness and asymmetry of effort and attention doom a relationship. If a wife goes out and becomes the family's bread-winner *and* does all the housework *and* raises the children *and* runs the errands *and* cooks the meals, sooner or later she will rebel. If the husband were in the same position, he'd rebel too. As soon as either partner starts to feel that the situation is unfair or uneven, it will begin to come apart. Alliances work like that.

There's always the danger that a partner is not really in it for the long haul. A British whisky company used a Japanese distributor until it felt it had gained enough experience to start its own sales operation in Japan. Japanese copier makers and automobile producers have done this to their American partners. It happens. There's always the danger that a partner is not really in it for the long run.

But the odds run the other way. There is a tremendous cost—and risk—in establishing your own distribution, logistics, manufacturing, sales, and R&D in every key market around the globe. It takes time to build skills in your own people and to develop good relations with vendors and customers. Nine times out of ten, you will want to stay in the alliance.

Inchicape, a British trading house with a strong regional base in Asia, distributes Toyota cars in China, Hong Kong, Singapore, elsewhere in the Pacific region, and several European countries. It also distributes Ricoh copiers in Hong Kong and Thailand. This arrangement benefits the Japanese producers, who get access to important parts of the world without having to set up their own distribution networks. It also benefits Inchicape, which can leverage its traditional British connections in Asia while adding new, globally competitive products to its distribution pipeline to replace the less attractive offerings of declining industries based in the United Kingdom.

In practice, though, companies involved in alliances often do start to have doubts. Say you've started up a Japanese alliance, not invested all that much, and been able to boost your production at home because of sales in Japan. Then you look at the actual cash flow from those sales, and it doesn't seem all that great. So you compare it with a competitor's results—a competitor who has gone into Japan entirely on its own. It's likely that you've forgotten how little effort you've put in when compared with the blood, sweat, and tears of your competitor.

All of a sudden you start to feel cheated; you remember every little inconvenience and frustration. You yield to the great temptation to compare apples with oranges, to moan about revenues while forgetting fixed costs. You start to question just how much the alliance is really doing for you.

It's a bit like going to a marriage counselor and complaining about the inconveniences of marriage because, had you not married, you could be dating anyone you liked. You focus on what you think you're missing and forget entirely about the benefits of being married. It's a psychological process. Alliance partners can fall into this kind of destructive pattern of thought, complaining about the annoyances of coordination, of working together, of not having free rein. They forget the benefits.

Actually, they forget to *look* for the benefits. And most accounting and control systems only make this worse. For instance, if you are running your own international sales operation in Japan, you know where to look for accurate measures of performance. You know how to read an income statement, figure out the return on invested capital, consolidate the performance of subsidiaries.

But when you're operating through a partner in Japan and you're asking yourself how that Japanese operation is doing, you forget to look for the benefits at home in the contribution to the fixed costs of R&D, manufacturing, and brand image. The financials don't highlight them; they usually don't even capture them. Most of the time these contributions—like the extra production volume for export to original equipment manufacturers—are simply invisible, below the line of sight.

Companies in the United States, in particular, often have large, dominant home-country operations. As a result, they report the revenues generated by imports from their overseas partners as their own domestic sales. In fact, they think of what they're doing not as importing but as managing procurement. Exports get recorded as overseas sales of the domestic divisions. In either case, the contribution of the foreign partner gets lost in the categories used by the American-based accounting system.

Even when alliances are good, companies can outgrow them. Needs change, and today's partner might not be the best or the most suitable tomorrow.

Financial institutions shift about like this frequently. If you're placing a major issue, you may need to tie up with a Swiss bank with deep pockets. If you need help with retail distribution, you may turn to Merrill Lynch or Shearson Lehman Hutton. In Japan, Nomura Securities may be the best partner because of its size and retail strength. You don't need to be good at everything yourself as long as you can find a partner who compensates for your weak points.

Managing multiple partners is more difficult in manufacturing industries, but it's still possible. IBM in the United States has a few important allies; in Japan it has teamed up with many. So many, in fact, a book has been published in Japanese entitled *IBM's Alliance Strategy in Japan.* * It has links with Ricoh in distribution and sales of low-end computers, with Nippon Steel in systems integration, with Fuji Bank in financial systems marketing, with OMRON in computer-integrated manufacturing, and with NTT in value-added networks. IBM is not a jack-of-all-trades. It has not made huge fixed-cost investments. In the eyes of Japanese customers, however, it has become an all-around player. For all practical purposes IBM Japan is like a mini-Mitsubishi group, with formal corporate relationships with nearly one thousand local companies as extensions of their sales, service, engineering, and manufacturing operations. No wonder IBM has achieved a major "insider" position in a fiercely competitive Japanese market, along with sales close to $8 billion and profits of $1.2 billion in 1988.

Every business arrangement has its useful life. But maintaining a presence in Japan by means of alliances *is* a permanent endeavor, an enduring part of IBM's strategy. And acting as if current arrangements are permanent helps them last longer. Just like marriage. If you start cheating on day two, the whole thing gets shaky fast.

Why does the cheating start? You're already pretty far down the slippery slope when you say to yourself, "I've just signed this deal with so-and-so to distribute my products. I don't need to

*Noriyoshi Miyamoto (Tokyo, Kodan-sha, 1988).

worry about that anymore as long as they send me my check on time." You're not holding up your half of the relationship. You're not working at it. More important, you're not trying to learn from it—or through it. You're not trying to grow, to get better as a partner. You've become a check casher, a coupon clipper. You start to imagine all sorts of grievances. And your eye starts to wander.

One of Japan's most remarkable success stories is 7-Eleven. Its success, however, is not due to the efforts of its American owner, Southland Corporation, but rather to the earnest acquisition of know-how by Ito-Yokado, the Japanese licensee. Faced with a takeover threat, Southland management collected something on the order of $5 billion through asset stripping and junk bond issues. The high interest cost of the leveraged buy-out caused the company to report a $6 million loss in 1987. Meanwhile, since the Japanese had completely absorbed the know-how for running 7-Eleven, the only thing Southland had left in Japan was its 7-Eleven brand.

When Southland's management asked Ito-Yokado to buy the brand name for half a billion dollars, Ito-Yokado's counter-proposal was to arrange an interest-free loan of 41 billion yen to Southland, in exchange for the annual royalty payment of $25 million, with the brand name as collateral. Should something happen to Southland so that it cannot pay back the debt, it will lose the brand and its Japanese affiliation completely. Yes, Southland got as much as half a billion dollars out of Japan in exchange for mundane know-how, so it should be as happy as a Yukon River gold miner. On the other hand, the loss of business connections in Japan means that Southland is permanently out of one of the most lucrative retail markets in the world.

Another company, an American media company, took 10 percent of the equity of a good ad agency in Japan. When the agency went public, the American investor sold off 3 percent and made a lot of money over and above its original investment. It still had 7 percent. Then the stockholders started to complain. At Tokyo's crazy stock market prices, that 7 percent represented about $40 million that was just sitting in Japan without earning dividends. So the stockholders pushed management to sell off the rest and bring the money back to the United States, where they could get at least a money-market level of return. No growth, of course. No lasting position in the booming Japanese market. Just a onetime killing.

Much the same logic seems to lie behind the sale by several American-based companies of their equity positions in Japanese joint ventures. McGraw-Hill (Nikkei-McGraw Hill), General Electric (Toshiba), B.F. Goodrich (Yokohama Rubber), CBS (CBS-Sony), and Nabisco (Yamazaki-Nabisco), among others, have all realized handsome capital gains in this fashion. If they had not given up their participation in so lucrative a market as Japan, however, the value of their holdings would now be many times greater still. GE, for example, probably realized more than $400 million from its sale of Toshiba shares during the early 1980s. But those same shares would be worth roughly $1.6 billion today. Similarly, B. F. Goodrich's investments in Yokohama Rubber would now be worth nearly $300 million, compared with an estimated $36 million that it realized from selling its shares during the late 1970s and early 1980s. Even more recently, needing to generate cash, Chrysler sold a large block of Mitsubishi Motors shares, and Honeywell much of its 50 percent stake in the very successful Yamatake-Honeywell joint venture in Japan. Of course, such funds have since found other opportunities for profitable investment, but they would have to do very well to offset the loss of so valuable an asset base in Japan.

This kind of equity-based mind-set makes the eye wander. It sends the message that alliances are not a desirable—or effective—means of coping with the pressures of globalization or of becoming a genuine insider throughout the Triad market. It reinforces the short-term orientation of managers already hard-pressed by the uncertainties of a new global environment.

When a dispute occurs in a transnational joint venture, it often has overtones of nationalism, sometimes even racism. Stereotypes persist. "Americans just can't understand our market," complain some frustrated partners. "The Germans are too rigid," complain others. "Those mechanical Japanese may be smart at home, but they sure as hell are dumb around here."

Much of the suspicion about these alliances, much of the hesitation and doubt, comes from the lurking suspicion that, whatever their appeal, their real effect will be to let the Japanese invaders into the American or the European house. In theory, runs the unstated concern, these alliances make sense. In practice, however, they are nothing but a Trojan horse. These days we are slower, dumber, and less hard-working than the Japanese. Give them an inch, give them any kind of access, and they will take over our markets for good.

This is dangerous thinking. Defeatism is infectious. If any managers are so convinced of their own laziness, stupidity, and sloth that they fear external contact through alliances, they will not have to wait for the Japanese to put them out of business. They are as good as dead already. Remember, the whole question of alliances comes up in the first place because such arrangements are demonstrably in the interests of both parties as they scramble to meet the demands of competing in a borderless world. If managers respond, Yes, we need them but we will certainly lose if we try them, they have lost already.

This fear of Trojan horses implies a management group's belief in its inability to structure an alliance intelligently or to execute it well. If this belief is colored by more than defeatism, if it is basically true, then the proper response should come not from defenders of alliances but from the market for corporate control.

Japanese companies have in fact ended relationships with partners. Toshiba's color TV joint venture in Britain is a good case in point. The British side did not deliver as promised, complaining that the unions would not go along and that local vendors were unable to comply with schedules and quality standards. Toshiba, with its eyes fixed on what it takes to be competitive in the global color TV market, could not accept that response. So it closed down the alliance and rebuilt its position on its own. It wanted the alliance to work. It believed that, properly managed, local vendors could reach world-class standards. And it was right. What it did not know was how to turn around a bad case of defeatism. And it should not be charged, in retrospect, with harboring Trojan horse–like motives because of that lack of knowledge.

There is nothing particularly Japanese about the failure of this alliance. Even with the best of intentions, sometimes alliances do not work out. Nor do Japanese firms looking to enter foreign markets always enter through such partnership arrangements. Sony, for instance, came into the United Kingdom entirely on its own. My point is that the relevant question for managers is not some imagined plot by companies in this or that part of the Triad. It is, rather, how best to satisfy customers and meet the challenges of global competition.

There are enough difficulties in meeting these challenges without imagining new ones. If managers have any doubts about carrying through an alliance, if they are not prepared to give it 100 percent of their best efforts—no matter what the reason— then they should not undertake it. My own view, discussed earlier, is clear: In most cases, doing it on your own is harder, more expensive, and more time-consuming than doing it with a suitable partner. But the benefits of an alliance remain benefits in theory only unless managers are willing to make the necessary effort. Nationalist suspicions do not help.

It does not take companies with radically different nationalities to have a "clash of cultures" in a collaborative effort. Most of the cross-border mergers that took place in Europe during the 1970s have resulted in divorce or in a takeover by one of the two partners. In Japan, mergers between Japanese companies—Dai-Ichi and Kangyo banks, for example—have journalists gossiping about personal conflicts at the top between factions in each company lingering on for ten years and more.

Good combinations—Ciba-Geigy and Nippon Steel (a combination of Yawata and Fuji), for example—are the exception, not the rule. Two corporate cultures rarely mesh well or smoothly. In the academic world there is a discipline devoted to the study of interpersonal relationships. To my knowledge, however, not one scholar specializes in the study of *intercompany* relationships. This is a serious omission, given the importance of joint ventures and alliances in today's global environment. We need to know much more than we do about what makes effective corporate relationships work.

Having been involved with many multicompany situations, I do not underestimate this task. We must recognize and accept the inescapable subtleties and difficulties of intercompany relationships. That is the essential starting point. Then we must focus not on contractual or equity-related issues but on the quality of the people at the interface between organizations. Finally we must understand that success requires frequent, rapport-building meetings on at least three organizational levels: top management, staff, and line management at the working level.

This is hard, motivation-testing work. No matter what they say, however, many companies don't really care about extending their global reach. All they want is to harvest the global market. They are not interested in the hard work of serving customers around the world. They are interested in next quarter's ROI. They are not concerned with getting back to strategy or delivering long-term value or forging entente. They are not serious about going global or about the painstaking work of building and maintaining the alliances a global market demands.

They may say all the right words and may even believe they really mean them. But most of the time they don't. For them it's only this year's fever or fashion. Last year, perhaps, it was quality circles. The year before, productivity. Now it's alliances and globalization. Preparing a company effectively for the partnerships necessary in a borderless economy is a decade-long process. Real, sustained, and committed effort is needed. But alliances are worth the effort. Properly managed alliances are among the best mechanisms that companies have found to bring strategy to bear in global markets.

9

"Lies, Damned Lies, and Statistics"

We can all recite the litany. The United States has a serious and, apparently, a structurally irremovable trade deficit with several of its major trading partners, especially Japan. For an economy so powerful, export levels for many categories of products are embarrassingly low. Unlike their European and Japanese counterparts, American-based firms have long been spoiled by the ready availability of a huge and wealthy domestic market. Most have little experience and even less interest in selling their wares abroad. No wonder the dollar has fallen to such dismal levels. The only surprise is that it hasn't gone lower still.

Meanwhile, me-generation consumers put virtually nothing away for a rainy day. Their motto is "Buy now and the hell with the future." Worse still, in their brand-name quest for instant gratification, the products they buy increasingly come from abroad. What all this means, of course, is that the country as a whole is on an irresponsible and unsustainable binge. It is throwing away in a few short years the economic abundance so painstakingly built up over many generations. And it is doing nothing to replace or replenish what now so quickly passes through its fingers. In fact, it is doing just about nothing to build up the reservoir of capital it needs to finance necessary investment. So it has to sell off its prime assets to foreign buyers and to borrow ever larger sums from abroad. Next year it will have to borrow even more to keep the party going—and to pay the interest on this year's celebration.

In happier times, when selfishness and short-term thinking did not so dominate the economic landscape, an implicit social contract meted out the economy's abundance to various constituencies fairly. Today, when everyone thinks only of himself, the disparities and inequalities keep rising. Companies chase inexpensive labor overseas and so "hollow out" their operations in the United States as rapidly as they can. The result is massive unemployment, which further drains the nation's resources by funneling scarce dollars from an already tiny investment pool into social transfer payments.

This is the portrait of an economy in the process of winding down. When it makes a few relatively feeble efforts to protest the advantages being taken of it by growth economies like Japan's, all it gets are promises, distortions, and delay. How long have we heard that Japan was going to open up this or that domestic market to American products? How long have we listened to Japanese officials tell us "It's very difficult" to carry out minute and altogether reasonable changes? How long are we going to keep giving away the store and, when the line of takers is not long enough, to keep going out and advertising for more? At long last, enough is enough.

We know this macroeconomic picture well, even the details. We don't like it at all, for it is anything but an encouraging picture, but we accept it, believe it, act upon it. We even applaud the analysts and commentators who explain it to us.

Falsehood of Statistics

Let's paint a different picture. The United States has no "foreign" trade. The United States never has to earn foreign currency to purchase something foreign. All it has to do is to expand its domestic economy to encompass its trading partners. If goods are bought by the United States from abroad, they are recorded as imports. After all, trade statistics measure goods that cross the national borders. However, because the money to buy these foreign goods is still denominated in dollars, buying them is no different from, say, buying California oranges or PCs from Texas. It makes no sense, then, to adjust the value of the dollar to "correct" the trade imbalance. That would be like printing more greenbacks to purchase the same amount of goods. If the need existed in the United States to purchase foreign goods, all adjusting the value of the dollar does is make the statistical measurement of imports (expressed in dollars) climb. It will not slow down the imports as long as comparable products are available in the United States.

As long as dollars are used as the settlement currency in foreign trade, the United States technically has no foreign trade. If, however, policymakers lower the value of the dollar in the belief that doing so will boost trade competitiveness, sooner or later the dollar will no longer be accepted by America's trading partners as settlement currency. This would be a very serious problem, for the United States would then borrow foreign money to pay for its excess imports. It is in America's best interest, therefore, to keep the dollar high. If a weaker currency promotes export, Argentina would be the strongest trading nation, says an analyst at Bear-Sterns.

Confused Negotiations

A few years ago Japan's former prime minister Yasuhiro Nakasone bowed once again to American complaints about the trade deficit. He made a speech to urge each of his fellow countrymen to buy at least $100 of imported American goods. So much for the idea of free trade. Nevertheless, if you needed a new tennis racket, you bought one made by Wilson. If you were out of ketchup, you bought some made by Del Monte. You picked up some tissues as long as you were going to the store—several boxes of Kleenex and Scotties. The problem, however, was that all these items had been made in Taiwan, Portugal, Hong Kong, and Japan.

These days, in a borderless world, it is difficult to tell what an "American" product is, because the very concept of an "American" or a "Japanese" or a "French" or a "German" product doesn't make sense. During the past several years American newspapers have been full of diatribes against Japanese restrictions on the import of beef from the United States. Here, at last, the critics say, is a clear case of a genuinely national product. There can be no question of outsourcing components from other countries. The only problem, however, is that Japanese cattle are raised almost entirely on American grain. The more Japanese beef eaten in Japan, the more American grain is consumed. Moreover, because grain agriculture has far higher levels of productivity in the United States than does cattle raising, the Americans are sure to win this race. If it becomes a matter of beef, then Americans must compete with Australia and Argentina, and in a much tougher game than grain.

That is not all. Because grain farmers in the United States are heavily subsidized by American taxpayers if their crops do not find adequate markets, the beef Japanese eat represents real savings to them. Not good enough, the critics reply. We want to ship American beef to Japan. Well, in 1989 about $841 million worth (or some 42 percent of total Japanese consumption) was shipped to Japan. But that number has to go up still more. Okay. Japanese importers such as Zenchiku Ltd. are aggressively buying up American ranches, feedlots, and packing plants. They and many other traders will soon be shipping in more beef from the United States than Americans do today, but it is not clear in what sense that represents a net increase in American exports. The beef export statistics from the United States will go up and the politicians and bureaucrats will be happy. But is this what the American people are really looking for?

In a borderless world, these kinds of trade figures are literally meaningless. Today some 1,300 American and European companies are operating in Japan in a significant way (that is, they are a subsidiary of one of the leading companies or they employ over three hundred people). Aggregated, their sales and earnings are immense. For example, according to McKinsey's foreign-affiliated companies (FAC) database, these FACs sales in 1987 were $260 billion, or 10.9 percent of Japan's GNP. None of their sales in Japan, however, show up as exports on the books of these other countries. American corporations' presence in Europe is roughly equivalent to one-fifth of European corporations' capitalization, were the Americans on the European stock market. Yet these heavy penetrations by the Americans in Europe and also in Japan do not appear in trade statistics.

Most competitive American corporations have "graduated" from the export phase and entered into a local insiderization phase. This is the single biggest reason why American exports have statistically declined. Moreover, the products they ship back home show up as Japanese or European exports to the United States. Texas Instruments (TI), for example, is the most competitive producer of memory chips in Japan. Not Hitachi or NEC. More than half of TI's annual production goes back to the United States via assembly operation in Singapore. The trade figures do not show this performance as boosting the overall trade balance of the American economy. Instead, it shows up as a significant increment to Japanese gross domestic product, Japanese exports, and U.S. imports.

These are just quirks of our accounting systems for trade, you say. In fact, they are worse than that. These are statistical conventions that bear no relation to the flows of economic activity in today's borderless world. But we act as if they were true, as if they really meant something. When the activities of only twenty companies account for roughly 50 percent of Japanese exports to the United States (and the activities of fifty companies for 75 percent), it matters greatly how we add up their numbers and which columns we put them in. Otherwise, they give too much room for politicians to make mistakes.

Trade is not a macroeconomic phenomenon any longer. It is what a rather small assembly of globally superior corporations do. In economist David Ricardo's world, when commodities were the major items of trade, price elasticity existed. So it made sense to adjust currency to balance trade. In today's world, what flows among developed countries are largely specialized products, not commodities. Currencies do not play a major role in the flows. Regardless of the exchange rate, Japan has to buy Boeing 747s from the United States; the United States has to buy audio-visual equipment from Japan.

Corporations have migrated to where their markets are, so what remains at home has a good reason to stay at home, and its sales take the form of exports. IBM and Xerox, for example, produce most of their goods in Japan and in Europe. They cannot easily switch production location every time currency fluctuates. The only way they can improve export competitiveness is to improve their own productivity and/or quality of their goods. Adjusting the currency is a completely wrong way to reduce the trade deficit.

Consumers have to pay for the idiosyncrasies of a government that reacts to the statistical trade imbalance issue with currency adjustments. Most American car companies raised their price tags when the imports had to raise theirs. They did not bother to boost their exports to Japan. The result: They have raked in profits and distributed them to shareholders and executives, not to customers.

The results of American corporations' migration across the border in search of lower production cost is larger than all of America's trade deficits with Canada and Mexico. The United States has not lost industrial competitiveness to these countries, as some now claim. The facts say otherwise, no matter how much some people would like to get the government's attention and assistance on R&D and capital expenditures.

In 1985 Japan exported (as we typically count the numbers) $95 billion worth of products to the United States and, in return, imported only $45 billion: a $50 billion deficit. But if we add to the total of Japan's imports the $55 billion worth of goods produced and sold by American companies in Japan (and add to

Japan's exports the $20 billion worth of products its companies made and sold in the United States), the trade figures would look quite different. Japan would then be seen to have consumed a total of $100 billion of American products; the United States, a total of $115 billion of Japanese products. The deficit picture disappears. What emerges is $200 billion of business activity between the most closely coupled trade pair in the world.

The deficit is an illusion created by accounting systems that are tragically out of date, systems that measure only the physical flow of goods across national borders. There was a time when such literal flows of goods from one country to the next were what trade was all about. A company produced something here and sold it there. Today, however, such physical movement of goods is only one—and often not even the most attractive— means by which companies make money. They license their technologies and receive risk-free royalties. They enter joint ventures and strategic alliances of various sorts. They outsource production. They produce in the countries where their markets are located. They own equity and receive dividends. Adam Smith–era statistics do not do justice to any of these now-standard means of doing business in the deregulated, borderless world.

Export/import numbers do not reflect at all the 70 percent or so of the American economy involved in service activities. They do bear some relation, of course, to the question of employment, but that is a different question. Nor do they confuse issues only between the United States and Japan. Components that American companies produce in their Canadian plants and bring back to the United States show up in the official statistics as Canadian exports. This is not a trade issue or a public policy issue. It is a company-specific question of manufacturing strategy and transfer pricing.

Admitting the truth can be awkward, especially for those who have been loudest in calling for drastic action to reverse a situation that does not actually exist. But awkwardness is preferable to allowing these misconceptions to persist and to infect what governments, as well as managers, do. We need new numbers that reflect real events, real flows of value. And we have to be prepared not to like what we find.

Consider 1985, the year the bilateral trade conflicts flared up. Add up Japanese purchases of American goods in that year (no matter where the goods were physically produced) and divide by the total Japanese population. The result: an average per capita consumption of some $580. This does not even include the substantial value of goods (roughly $40 billion) produced under American license in Japan, such as Coca-Cola and McDonald's. Now add up American purchases of Japanese goods (no matter where produced) and divide by the total American population. The result: an average per capita consumption of $298. Who should buy $100 or more of whose goods?

One problem that comes up is the poor ability of the Japanese government to discuss and explain these new perspectives on trade to the American trade negotiators and to the Japanese people in general—what is called "public relations" in the United States. Such a function was never needed in Japan, where the government had the tacit understanding of its people on whatever it did. There is no question Japan has many explicit and implicit trade barriers. But most American companies have overcome these and in general are enjoying enormous success. Those who did not succeed normally end up in Washington complaining about market access and the nontariff barriers.

This becomes obvious if you trace the origin of the U.S.–Japan trade disputes. Most of them have been initiated by a small company whose products and/or services were not readily accepted by the Japanese consumers complaining to the local senator or congressman. Semiconductor disputes are particularly comical. The strongest American chip producers are already well integrated into the Japanese marketplace. Many Japanese companies are already producing in the United States. The largest American producers—IBM and AT&T—mainly produce for their internal use, hence do not contribute to the export statistics. It is therefore nonsense that the Japanese government agreed to increase the American imports to roughly 20 percent of Japanese chip consumption. The United States does not produce chips for consumer electronics, which is the main requirement of the Japanese. Now the Ministry of International Trade and Industry is calling on each Japanese company to come up with a list of American companies for chip procurement and to boost imports to more than 20 percent of purchases. And American producers are turning these orders down because they are too busy to fill their orders at home.

Finally, the bureaucrats agreed to include those chips produced in Japan by American companies, such as TI, and those produced by the Japanese under license from the United States, such as Intel microprocessors by Hitachi. Such governmental solutions do not change the trade statistics. They are deceiving the public because they cannot deliver the target, which is set based on a completely wrong understanding of the trade statistics.

Empty Pockets?

Trade is not the only part of the conventional macroeconomic "house" that is rotting. Consider, for example, the "fact" that self-indulgent Americans mortgage their future while the ever-industrious Japanese squirrel away money that can be used to fuel industrial development. According to the most recent government statistics, the Japanese savings rate is 16.6 percent and the American rate, 4.3 percent. On both sides of the Pacific, policies are formulated on the assumption that these saving statistics are correct.

Macroeconomists and government negotiators say Americans should save much more. This would reduce the U.S. current account deficit, which they say is caused by the investment/savings imbalance and the government fiscal deficit. In Japan the government has approved the Maekawa Report, proposing that Japan become a consuming giant like the United States. The current overheating of the Japanese economy, particularly in real estate and construction, is the result of the government's emergency spending of $42 billion as urged by the report and the U.S. government.

Few policymakers have looked into the assumptions behind the savings statistics, despite their influence. Savings rates are defined as disposable income minus consumption, divided by disposable income. Japan's statistics are based on an accounting system advocated by the United Nations. The American figures are based on its own system, administered by the Commerce Department. The two are significantly different; if one converts the U.S. statistics to the international measure, the American savings rate jumps to 6.8 percent instead of 4.3 percent.

The savings rates move closer still if you remove discrepancies such as, for example, the treatment of public pensions. The American system treats it as savings of the government rather than of the private sector. In fact, if you took out all the accounting inconsistencies, the difference in savings rate between Japan and the United States would be 5.7 percentage points instead of 12.3. That is still a significant difference, but not nearly as big as is generally perceived.

When I published this analysis in the *Japan Economic Journal* in April 1988, it seemed to surprise both government and the private sector. However, the Bank of Japan later circulated a bulletin confirming my calculation and updating the data base.* After adjusting for the recent appreciation in Tokyo stock prices and removing some American elements for which no Japanese equivalents were available, the Bank of Japan put the U.S. savings rate at 14.7 percent and the Japanese rate at 16.7 percent, a mere 2.0-percentage-point difference.

Moreover, the 5.7- or 2.0-percentage-point gap can be erased if you consider the sociocultural differences between Japan and the United States. For example, assume that you buy a house in the United States for $200,000 and invest another $200,000 for renovation. The former is counted as savings by the U.S. government and the latter as consumption. However, when you sell the

---

Tokeigeppo (Statistical Monthly), Bank of Japan, July 1988.

house, you hope to sell it for $400,000 or more. This means that some "consumption" (such as home renovation) actually is another form of savings. Even an automobile has some residual value in the United States, and not all that "consumption" actually has been consumed. The resale value acts like your savings "in case of an emergency." Most consumer durables are classified as consumption, but they have significant residual values.

In Japan, for cultural reasons, "consumption" such as housing renovation is not appreciated by the next buyer or the real estate agent, and only the land is assessed as having value. A newly built house has zero value after only five years. Hence, money invested in housing construction and renovation is truly consumed and not saved at all. The same is true for automobiles, because there isn't an attractive resale market in Japan.

In general, the differences make it easier for Americans to "buy now and pay later." In fact, Americans can consume aggressively to save. This practice makes the American consumption statistics higher than reality. Conversely, because consumption does not yield as much residual value in Japan, the Japanese must "save to buy" goods and houses. In truth, Americans and Japanese both end up buying and owning pretty much the same things at the same rates. If you add savings to consumer credit, the combination is about the same percentage of disposable income in both countries, 29 percent. The only difference is the timing of payment. Even though the amount of consumption may be the same, the Japanese method tends to show higher savings in the bank first, while the American method shows a negative in the bank because Americans borrow from the future. The point is both end up buying about the same amount.

Conservatism on the part of Japanese banks contributes to this difference. On average, they require 25 percent to 33 percent down for the purchase of a house, compared with the 10 percent to 20 percent typically required by American banks. If Japanese banks reduced their requirements, the remaining difference in savings would close completely. Of the 16.6 percent Japanese savings rate, 7.9 percent goes toward home downpayments.

Contributing also is the traditional American tax deductibility of interest on borrowings. This leads Americans to take out loans rather than exhaust savings to buy durables. In Japan the incentive is reversed. Interest earnings on the savings up to a certain amount can be tax exempt. When this disparity in tax treatment is taken into account, the statistical savings gap should close or even reverse.

What I am trying to prove is that the Japanese and the Americans don't have much different attitudes toward consumption. What they are doing is responding differently to the inherent differences in tax and other systems in their countries. Changing the tax laws would result in a completely different macroeconomic picture with the same people. For example, if the Japanese banks accepted a lower downpayment and the secondary housing market appreciated used houses much more fairly, any statistical savings gap between Japan and the United States would disappear altogether.

It can even be argued that Americans save *more* than Japanese. All of the conventional savings statistics are based on "flow," or year-to-year savings over discretionary income. However, real savings should be defined as how much you have in "stock." In 1985 when the Maekawa Report was written, the financial assets of the U.S. personal sector were $7.87 trillion. Japan's were $2.24 trillion. This translates into financial assets of $33,000 per capita for the United States and $18,000 for Japan. Americans have more assets in savings, insurance, pensions, and securities than Japanese, who favor their famous "tax-free" time deposits.

The big asset base in the United States translates into a new increase in financial assets of some $500 billion annually, compared with only $176 billion in Japan. On average, American financial instruments perform 4 percent to 5 percent better than those in Japan. This spread further increases the asset base of Americans year in and year out. During 1981 to 1985, the American savings rate measured on the financial asset base was 19.6 percent, compared with 14.4 percent for the Japanese.

You can argue, using a variety of differences in social systems, habits, cultural and statistical treatment, but it all seems to lead to one conclusion: There is not much difference in the *real* savings of Americans and Japanese. This is shocking, because the Japanese government has promised the United States and the rest of the world that "We'll become a consuming superpower from a savings nation." Based on the wrong statistics, we adopt the wrong policies. That is why trade and other statistics do not "improve," even though the Japanese implement "action programs" earnestly.

Assets and Liabilities

Another part of the argument that is false is that the debt side of the national balance sheet in the United States has ballooned while the asset side has virtually dried up. While President Ronald Reagan was in the White House, America slipped from owning the world's largest assets overseas to bearing the largest liabilities. This reversal gained the United States the image of being a profligate spender and caused many politicians and economists to wring their hands. They point to the fact that it took the United States over sixty years to build up its assets and only eight years of Mr. Reagan's "strong America" policy to wipe them all out.

But let's look at the figures, in particular at the $400 billion increase in American liabilities between 1981 and 1986 that caused the country's net assets to go from plus $141 billion to minus $264 billion. What do these statistics prove and disprove about Reagan's policies and the health of the American economy? Is the country really living on blank checks?

First of all, during the same five-year period, overseas assets owned by American corporations and individuals did not decrease. In fact, they increased steadily from $720 billion to $1.07 trillion from 1981 to 1986. Foreign-owned assets in the United States during the same period increased sharply, from $580 billion to $1.38 trillion. It's the latter development that led to the negative $264 billion in 1986 in America's external liabilities.

These investments in the United States from overseas soared

primarily for three reasons: the trade deficit, dollar depreciation, and the availability of high-performing instruments in the nation. The dollars accumulated by America's trading partners eventually must be used to buy something in the United States. When these purchases are made, the U.S. government statistically records them as foreign-owned assets at home. But how do these "liabilities" hurt the United States? Unlike Brazil, which must borrow dollars if it cannot pay accepted currency for international settlements, the United States can settle them in dollars. What is troublesome for Brazil is that if its currency loses value, as it has, the dollars become more expensive. The same kind of debt spiral is not likely to happen in the United States.

What's more, Uncle Sam pays the same amount of interest to all investors in government securities. It makes no difference if he has to pay interest to an Arkansas farmer, a British fund manager in New York, or a Japanese housewife in Osaka. They all get dollars. The amount of dollars of interest contributes to the federal budget deficit, but it is not a special problem of "external" liabilities. More important, although most foreign investments in the United States—for example, real estate and companies—are recorded at the national border as external liabilities, they are not interest-bearing. This means that the United States does not have to pay for its "external liabilities."

The United States is an attractive place to invest. Japan does not have the equivalent of leveraged-buyout funds producing 40 percent yields, junk bonds yielding 20 percent, government securities at 9.5 percent, and savings accounts at 6.5 percent. Most Japanese money sits in postal savings and time deposits at 4 percent at best. The Swiss and the Germans have the same problem, and they too invest in the United States. Wealthy people in developing countries also see the United States as a high-yielding haven. Just as in the case of an attractive company in which everyone wants to invest, money pours into the United States. Nothing is wrong with this. It is the normal behavior of an exchangeable commodity, money. Because what are invested in are called "external liabilities," people worry.

The Plaza agreement in 1985 accelerated this process of investment. At the strong request of U.S. Treasury Secretary James Baker, the value of the dollar was lowered to make American industrial goods more competitive. This was a strategy focused only on the nation's trade deficit. As discussed earlier, you cannot, however, make only certain things cheaper when you adjust a country's exchange rate. American grains and scientific instruments may have become more competitive externally by making the dollar cheaper, but so have American real estate, companies, and buildings. So, to take advantage of these bargains, foreign countries are now investing even more dollars than they accumulated through trade.

Of the $400 billion of recorded increases in the external liabilities of the United States, as much as $350 billion are these kinds of investments, not interbank borrowings, as they are with Brazil. Nevertheless, some patriotic American economists caution against the danger of "capital flight." They say that if the United States is so dependent on foreign investments and capital to get its economic engine going, it is vulnerable to foreigners and their will to keep it going. If confidence in the United States drops and foreign money stops coming in, the market will dry up and interest rates will skyrocket, so they argue.

It is hard to believe this argument, which puts the blame on the foreign investors per se. Americans have an $8 trillion stock of money in the private sector. The U.S. government is always in need of foreign capital to buy its securities, because Americans are not content with the 9 percent interest that government securities typically pay. They seek higher-yielding instruments. If they were willing to accept lower interest rates, the nation's "dependence on foreign capital" would not exist.

There is a danger of capital flight, all right. If the United States ceases to be an attractive place to invest, Americans will be the first to find better homes for their money. American pension-fund managers and investment bankers know the world well and have to be fast on their feet to satisfy their investors. They are not going to sit on mediocre results. When it comes to money, they and many American investors are going to behave as if they have no nationality. Money, be it American or foreign, will freely migrate in and out of the artificial national borders.

In today's global financial market, money finds the best and the most comfortable place to live. For those economists worried about external liabilities, there is a solution: Have the market crash. American money will gush out of the country. And the bureaucrats and old-style statisticians will happily measure and record a surge in American external assets. A safer course, one that won't erase the growth in liabilities but will nevertheless enable the United States to prosper, is to keep the dollar strong and stable. Money flows into the United States because it is an attractive market. The nation and its friends should begin to worry if that flow stops.

Hollow Men?

Trade figures do not prove a loss of American prowess. Even though steel has lost its competitiveness and autos are still struggling, the United States is still the largest exporter of manufactured goods. If you add up all exports worldwide, the United States continues to capture 18 percent, compared with 13 percent for West Germany and 12 percent for Japan.

But that is not the way companies keep score. There is no business Olympics. American multinationals don't operate like home-country amateurs for the sake of balancing trade statistics. They are world-class because they operate worldwide. Because of them, the American share of manufactured goods exported from other countries is increasing. It was 13 percent in 1977, 14 percent in 1983, and 15 percent of the worldwide third-country trade in 1985. When American companies move abroad, they not only sell to local markets but become big exporters—often back to the United States. Almost 20 percent of American imports come from American affiliates overseas.

Critics of American companies point to their production abroad and talk about lost jobs. It's true that American multinationals employ 8.3 million people overseas. But there is no evidence of the "hollowing out" of the United States in the manufacturing sector. America's share of all manufacturing jobs in the United States, Japan, Europe, and the newly industrializing countries was 27 percent in 1960. It reached 30 percent in 1980, and was still at 30 percent in 1986, when many cover stories decried the hollowing out of America or the decline of American manufacturing competitiveness. Meanwhile, Europe's share of these jobs declined from 51 percent in 1960 to 32 percent in 1986. Europe, not the United States, is being hollowed out by the NIEs and Japan.

The United States looks as if it is being hollowed out only when you compare its manufacturing sector with its even more dynamic service sector. Between 1960 and 1986 jobs in manufacturing declined to 24 percent of all jobs from 34 percent, while jobs in the service sector increased to 73 percent from 56 percent. So we know that this phenomenon is relative within the United States, not without.

That's the good news. The bad news is that not many of those 8.3 million jobs will move to the United States as a result of the weakened dollar. Politicians, of course, want them to. Many American multinationals do not. They moved abroad for several good reasons: to get close to markets they sell in, to get good ideas from their foreign customers, to avoid protectionism, and to get products and components that were better or cheaper. They were not forced to go abroad simply because the dollar was overvalued. That became a factor only recently. American companies have been gradually increasing their presence abroad for decades.

In the early 1960s McKinsey analyzed the overseas role and investments of one hundred major American industrial corporations. Between 1950 and 1960 their foreign sales increased from 10 percent to 17 percent of total business. Four out of five companies doubled their overseas sales; 75 percent more than doubled their foreign assets. While the exports of half these companies more than doubled from 1950 to 1960, their total overseas production increased substantially more than their exports. In 1950 the median company in this group produced almost two-thirds of its overseas sales volume in the United States. By 1960 that figure dropped to 30 percent. McKinsey's 1983 study of midsize growth companies shows this same push to move production close to markets, indicating that the drive to overseas production begins at a relatively early stage of the company's growth in size. Since the 1950s jobs have been created by overseas markets as much as they have been "lost" to them.

As described in Chapter 6, American companies have followed a five-stage evolution of expansion abroad during that same time.* Stage 4 and stage 5 companies can do something that may foil predictions about the cheap dollar bringing production back to the United States. As exchange rates have become increasingly volatile, those companies have learned how to diffuse currency risk with financial manipulations rather than switching production base back and forth. This is the key reason why trade flows are slow to respond to currency shifts.

Top-tier Japanese corporations have virtually *neutralized* the impact of currency fluctuations by trying almost everything they could think of—matching revenues and costs in major currencies, producing in NIEs (which have "in-between" currencies), importing as much as they export, excelling in financial engineering *("zaitech")* and currency trading, differentiating/changing models frequently to raise prices, and pressuring suppliers to share currency gains. As a result, they have survived the huge change in the dollar/yen relationship over the past decade.

Well-run American and European companies have advanced far beyond these tactics. They make decisions about ownership and finance not only to hedge their currency exposure but to take advantage of significant differences in tax rates and treatment of income. They also take advantage of new opportunities to control

*For a complete explanation, see my *Beyond National Borders* (Homewood, IL, Dow Jones-Irwin, 1987).

rather than own assets. Japanese CEOs are now joining the club. Ten years ago dinner parties were spoiled when someone slipped in a note saying the dollar declined by one yen. That would have been a loss of a few million dollars income annually. Today a CEO wouldn't even stop playing golf when the dollar goes up or down by 10 yen. If the dollar goes up, the Japanese can export more. If it goes down, the Japanese can buy American assets cheaply. Currency fluctuations have simply given CEOs and their companies wider options in global strategy.

More broadly, developments in borderless financial markets in general have given them more options than they had a decade ago. When they make plans they try to use these options to balance the value of flexibility against other factors such as protectionism, likely local inflation rates, shifts in the value of local currency, presence of leading-edge customers, quality and education of the work force, and importance of economies of scale. Despite the dollar's big slide, they are not going to drop their plans and move production back to the United States overnight. The ILE is the world-leading edge that corporations see and the one politicians, bureaucrats, and traditional macroeconomists miss.

Companies have tried to make their production more mobile, often by using suppliers worldwide as well as by building plants with low "break-evens." It is likely that both American and non-American firms will consider producing more in the United States, particularly if labor relations continue to improve. The advantages of being inside the American market are considerable. After all, it is the world's largest market and has some of the choosiest customers, with tough and smart competitors.

However, old-fashioned economic policies make the executives remain skeptical. Foreign companies are hesitant to boost their investment in the United States for fear that the dollar will drop even more, diminishing the relative value of any new assets. In order not to realize the loss, only older investments are kept in dollars. Senior managers worry that the weaker dollar will ignite inflation in the United States if oil prices go up, imported goods are gradually replaced by domestic production, and the interest on U.S. government securities is raised to attract the influx of foreign capital. They also worry that Congress may introduce all kinds of internal, navel-watching bills. The stop-and-go economic policies of the mightiest government in the world are the reason why the United States has not become a stable world champion for production.

Chasing cheap currencies is about as bad an international business strategy as chasing cheap labor. We have learned the prudence of this lesson thanks to the volatility of currency created mainly by politicians and bureaucrats with bad macroeconomic advisors. Leapfrogging from country to country isn't very profitable in the end. The reality is that the United States will need a stronger and more stable dollar before its own companies reverse their long-term trend of moving production overseas.

10

The FX Empire

Nowhere is the cost of failed or incomplete perception higher than in the distorted but still widely held view of the basic nature of international economic activity. When managers think of this activity, they usually think in terms of goods being traded across national borders. In 1988 the total volume of these flows within the Triad amounted to $600 billion *annually.* By contrast, the *daily* volume in foreign exchange (FX) trading amounted to $600 billion. These exchange transactions began as a means to smooth and facilitate the flows of traditional trade and investment. But this FX "tail" has grown to be some hundred times larger than the original trade "dog."

Each day a few billion dollars' worth of goods changes hands across national borders. On the same day the key money markets of New York, Tokyo, and London process FX transactions worth several hundred billions of dollars. Faced with this kind of evidence, no one can argue that FX trading is still a mere adjunct to other forms of economic activity. It is an end in itself. It obeys rules of its own and displays its own distinctive forms of behavior. Economic analyses that for years made reasonable sense of trade in goods cannot explain, say, a 40 percent annual fluctuation in the exchange rates between two currencies when the fundamentals of the underlying economies have changed very little. Something else, something different, is going on here, and it needs to be understood.

The Brave New World of FX

Between March 19, 1986, and January 29, 1987, the Bank of Japan injected $16 billion into the currency markets to arrest the dollar's free fall—a bit more than half during the first two and one-half weeks of 1987 alone. Nothing happened. Central bankers have always been slow to bring out their heavy guns, not wanting to cause disruptions in the financial markets. Here, even the largest field pieces had virtually no effect. The FX market had become an empire of its own, no longer vulnerable even to the actions of determined governments. It did not obey the laws everyone thought still controlled it.

The FX market is unleashed because financial markets in the Triad are basically deregulated and interlinked. Analyses based on traditional ideas of purchasing power between nations cannot begin to explain the current yen/dollar exchange-rate behaviors. This is true in part because the Japanese system of distribution is much less efficient than that of the United States, and the end user price does not necessarily reflect the landed cost, known as CIF. Policy analysts in Washington are gradually finding this out, but anyone who has shopped in both the United States and Japan knows it well. If you walk into the 47th Street Photo Shop in New York, you can buy a Japanese-made camera or PC for substantially less than it would cost at Yodobashi Camera in Tokyo. American consumers are delighted. Politicians looking for votes cry foul.

This is dumping, isn't it, or something pretty darn close? By the laws of economics most of those politicians learned in school, at least the ones they remember, New York prices cannot be lower at the same time that the exchange rate has moved so strongly against the dollar. Traditionally, differences in purchasing power were believed to influence exchange rates in order to equalize prices. Something fishy, therefore, must be going on. But international trade is based on a product's landed cost, not its end user price. Price elasticities that, in theory, should follow directly from changes in exchange rates will not occur if the ultimate decision-making consumer is insulated from their effects.

If a weak dollar allows an American maker of scientific instruments to offer Japanese customers a better delivered price, then its market share will rise. If a strong yen forces a Japanese camera maker to offer New Yorkers a less attractive delivered price, then its share will fall. In most consumer electronics and office automation equipment, manufacturing cost is usually less than 30 percent of list price. Currency affects only this smaller portion. So if the FX effects get eaten up and more by the costs of domestic distribution in Japan, then the price tags on Japanese goods on American retail shelves can in fact be lower than those on the same goods in Tokyo. The exchange rate is where it is for other reasons. It does not reflect comparative purchasing power. So the desire of politicians and central bankers to reduce the trade deficit through fiddling with the currency hasn't worked.

What has happened is that the FX market has become an extremely attractive arena for investment in its own right. Politicians and economists who tried to use FX to fix trade succeeded only in making it more attractive to speculative FX traders. If you look back over ten years' history of monthly fluctuations in the dollar/yen rate, you will readily see that, with few exceptions, the rate has moved more than 1 percent each month. In fact, the average has been closer to 4.5 percent. This adds up to an average annual fluctuation of well over 50 percent. The opportunities to make money are plentiful. There are many other high-yield opportunities for investment—real estate, precious metals, stocks, and even (in Japan) golf club memberships. But capital gains here often get heavily taxed, and the markets are heavily regulated. They are also finite. No such limits trouble the universe of FX.

At the root of these developments is the recent explosion of superliquidity in the Triad's financial markets. In Japan, for example, private savings and the corporate sector generate more than $1 billion in surplus capital *every day* that has to be invested somewhere. Real consumption—more plants, more equipment—can absorb only so much. And virtually all of that can be financed with the cash flow generated by the depreciation of past capital investments. Nor do Japanese companies have to pay out dividends to the extent American companies do. The rest of the money really does have to find another "bucket" to sit in. For the major players, the institutional investors, it matters very little which buckets get chosen—so long as they offer a competitive return and are interchangeable (that is, tradable).

In Japan the stock market has become an increasingly less attractive bucket. It is already filled up with more water (excess liquidity)—at an average price/earnings ratio (P/E) of 80—than logical minds can comprehend or accept. Real estate is little better. Prices in central Tokyo have risen three to five times during the past several years. This bucket is already so uncomfortably full that the payback period for a new downtown office building is regularly figured at more than one hundred years, and rental income, which runs 1 or 2 percent of investment, does not even begin to cover the 4 or 5 percent interest that has to be paid to the bank, compared with a 7 to 8 percent return in the American office buildings. No one minds that much because they all expect property values to keep doubling every few years. Surely this is unrealistic.

Yet, where else to look? At the Kasumigaseki Country Club, membership fees to play golf there run on the order of $2 million—a figure that would be entirely inexplicable if the memberships could not be traded, which indeed they are. There is not much space left below the rim of this bucket either. Still, the money has to go somewhere. And there is more of it every day, as individuals and companies borrow at very low rates to make further investments against the inflated value of their equity and real estate holdings, expecting appreciation faster than inflation and cost of money combined.

That "somewhere" is the autonomous FX empire. Governments have, of course, tried to regulate it, to bring its movements under better control. Since Bretton Woods and the end of fixed currency rates, however, every time there have been official efforts to stablize FX, the volatility of the world's monetary system has become greater. Volatility offers speculators a better chance to make money, and FX is a speculator's paradise. The more money they make, the more attractive FX seems and the bigger—and still more lucrative—its empire becomes. No other investment bucket can offer anything like its attractions.

There is little risk of exposure to legal troubles in FX, such as insider trading in the stock market or restraints on investment of the kind imposed by Glass-Steagall. There is a low, virtually nonexistent, barrier to entry. Current data available to any PC user through Reuters, Quotron, Telerate, and the like can turn novice investors into wealthy individuals (and vice versa) in short order. Larger financial institutions—Japanese banks, trading houses, and insurance firms, for example—already make more money from their FX activities than from their traditional lines of business. In the United States these institutions can participate directly in lucrative stock or real estate transactions. In Japan this is more difficult, as the market is divided and protected for the specialist—for example, stocks for the brokers and real estate transactions are heavily taxed. FX, however, is broadly available to anyone who wants to play. Even old-line manufacturers got into the act, purchasing futures and options to protect their export/import transactions. However, they, like the financial institutions, are now finding this new line of FX business to be more profitable than the old line of trading goods.

This FX empire has rendered obsolete much of the way we used to think about macroeconomics. In a fundamental sense, money supply has moved well beyond the control of any single government. There are dollar- and yen-based markets everywhere. The global, interlinked, tradable FX empire allows money literally to travel around the globe in seconds. Even if, for instance, the Bank of Japan decides to tighten up the money supply at home, desired funds are instantaneously available from abroad. During 1988 more funds were raised in Europe than at home for the entire Japanese private sector. Further, the conventional metrics that we have long applied to measure inflation—the consumer and wholesale price indices—no longer count for much. In the past, overliquidity resulted in inflation as excess money bought up available inventory, for example, in expectation of higher prices. But today's oversupply of commodities and industrial goods makes investments in goods very risky. Thus superliquidity is contained in tradable buckets, and very little has leaked out to drive prices up. No thanks to government policy, the FX bucket is accommodatingly large and expandable at need. The ILE also is acting as a very kind mechanism to dilute any government's mistakes. For example, if one government oversupplies the money, it can leak out to the rest of the ILE and cause less serious inflation at home, as is the case of the "homeless" dollars in Europe. Inflation disappeared because of the interchangeable buckets of FX, real estate, stocks, rather than clever governmental policies. There is no apparent limit to supply—that is, to what it can absorb. Thus inflation indices that are an aggregate price of goods can remain stable while real estate and stock prices soar. The deregulated financial market has created a gigantic sponge to absorb inflation that would have come for sure due to the free-wheeling money-printing policies of most governments.

At the same time, the opportunities to make profits through FX-based speculation have diminished the importance of interest rates. Governments, however, especially that of the United States, still importune their trading partners to keep interest rates low. Even as the spread in rates between Japan and Germany, on the one side, and the United States, on the other, widened to as much as 5 to 6 percent during 1988–89, the falling value of the dollar made the spread too small to attract money from either.

When profit-making opportunities on the exchange rates themselves near 50 percent or so a year, there is little that the spread in interest rates can do to make interest-bearing investments attractive. If the decline of the value of the dollar stopped for sure, there will be unstoppable forces to drive up its value, as the United States is a preferred haven for most investors.

Even though governments cannot "manage" the FX empire in the same ways they have long tried to manage other dimensions of macro policy, they can certainly affect it. The relative performance of national economies—the "fundamentals"—do not change rapidly. They do not fluctuate wildly from day to day, or shift 40 or 50 percent in a year. But exchange rates do. What drives them? A check of the Reuters and Telerate services suggests that it is the explicit and implicit comments of government officials, particularly American government officials, that drive many of these changes.

On a real-time basis, traders pay more attention to announcements (or hints) about fundamentals than to the fundamentals themselves. FX information services carry most of their information in English. As a result, a trader's "share of mind," which is dominated by the weighted average psychology of other traders' interpretations of how rates are likely to move, is disproportionately influenced by news or hints of shifting policies in the United States.

Something dramatic has happened in the world of economics. It was not caused by the two energy crises. It was not caused by the summits. It is the result of technological breakthroughs in the communication industry and of financial deregulation in the major industrial economies. Currencies started to move like a yo-yo. In the past currency fluctuated to reflect the relative purchasing power of nations. Financial fundamentals prevailed. Differences among nations in the rates of interest and inflation were adjusted so as to make the return on investment nearly equal in interlinked economies.

Politicians and macroeconomists, not fully understanding this, started to intervene in the natural flow of money. Today "political paradigms," not fundamentals, have become the major force influencing exchange rates. When Reagonomics called for a "strong America through a strong dollar," the dollar got strong. When James Baker argued that the strong dollar was the cause of the nation's lost competitiveness and hence of its trade deficit, the dollar declined against the yen almost to one-half (from 240 to 120 yen to the dollar) in the year after the Plaza agreement.

While this deficit continued, "America"—not American products—became very competitive. Foreign capital rushed into the United States to buy anything American, ranging from a Firestone Tire Company to a La Costa Country Club. It is obvious that such assets are tradable and that currency exchange rates must reflect the purchasing power of these assets, as well as of traditional goods. But this simple logic has been completely neglected by the economists who have advocated adjusting the dollar downward to restore America's export competitiveness—a very narrow definition of trade indeed. Exchange rates must be adjusted to reflect investment opportunities of anything tradable across the border, ranging from goods to assets, from real money to futures, options, and rights.

If you look, for example, at only semiconductors and automobiles, the correct exchange rate may be 100 yen to a dollar. However, if you look at the real estate price of Tokyo and its financial power relative to, say, Manhattan, anything below 300 yen to a dollar is a bargain exchange rate. If you look at the proper rate of return on financial investments, the dollar will have to become a few percentage points weaker against the yen every year if the current spread of the interest rates is to be kept in place. Considering all these different forces at work, the dollar should be a lot higher than where it is now, which is 140 yen.

Unless this is corrected, there will be a surge of foreign capital into the United States, and that will not stop at Treasury bonds and bills and real estate, but will creep into every corner of the American economy. This is not all bad. Japanese investment is a stabilizing force in the American economy because it is long-term oriented and not dependent on quick, high-risk opportunities for excessive returns. Still, it is not clear to me if this flood of investment from around the world is what American people really want, although that is clearly what American officials are encouraging.

A Home for Scoundrels

By all relevant measures, then, the FX empire is a critical new fact of macroeconomic life. No firm operating on more than a purely local scale can afford to shape its strategy without paying that empire the most careful attention. So much is common sense. FX has to be taken seriously. It is a standard to which all responsible managers must now flock. Under that same banner, however, also march some very unwelcome characters. These are the policymakers—and the managers—who see in FX a means to redress perceived imbalances in trade.

In the past, when political leaders found themselves bankrupt of effective policy and no longer able to rally their people, they would wave the flag and try to stir up emotions by appeals to patriotic sentiment. Patriotism thus embraced, wrote Dr. Johnson long ago, was the last refuge of the scoundrel. The pose was fair-seeming, the sentiment noble but easily perverted to improper ends. So today with trade and the magic wand of FX adjustments. The call to right great wrongs by letting the dollar fall or rise has popular appeal. It wins votes. It makes the enemy concrete and reachable and recommends a weapon that lies ready. It promises relief from an adversity that is neither well understood nor felt to be just. As policy, however, it is misguided. And as the official position of leaders, it is irresponsible.

There was a time, in the days of David Ricardo and Adam Smith, when the goods traded internationally were primarily commodities, such as cotton, wine, and wool. Raw materials and labor accounted for a disproportionate share of their cost. If governments fiddled with exchange rates, never an exact science, the results were at least directionally predictable. As recently as fifteen years ago, Japan did still compete with the

United States in such manufactured commodity goods as steel, plastics, fertilizers, and textiles. But not today. Today the competition is in more advanced manufactured goods, where the cost structure is quite different. Even if precise fiddling were possible, it would not have the desired effect. And in this area precision is not position.

Most of the talk about FX manipulation is aimed at Japan. This is the result, in part, of people being taken in by a set of statistics about trade. But it also reflects a blindness both about the product categories in which the United States and Japan compete and about the relative insensitivity of those categories to shifts in exchange rates. Many of the products that Japan exports to the United States today are the survivors of the FX volatility—video recorders, for example, or compact disc players or memory chips or high-end cassette players, cameras, ceramic components, and NC machines or large-screen television sets. These products do not compete with American products because there are few, if any, with which to compete.

The Japanese corporations, moreover, are very good at segmenting markets and then forging an entry in segments where there is relatively little competition—usually from the low end initially, but then in the high end, as in cameras and motorbikes. FX adjustments would have had to be immense to affect these strategies. And if they had been, what about the sacrifice in American consumer welfare that would have resulted? Where do we measure in the value, now lost to American consumers, of having had access to products in categories no one else was really serving?

Even here we are talking about sophisticated manufactured products, which are relatively FX insensitive, and not commodity products, such as agriculture, which are FX sensitive. But even in agriculture, the conventional logic doesn't work because, scare headlines in the business press aside, American farmers are *not* in competition with Japanese farmers. So if the United States wants to make its agricultural products more competitive in Japan and if it is determined to do so by playing with exchange rates, then its leaders still make a logical error by tampering with the dollar/

yen rate. American farmers compete with farmers in Australia, Thailand, China, and Brazil for most of their products to be sold in Japan. Japan imports more than 60 percent of all American beef and veal sold abroad, more than 30 percent of all feed grains and corn, and close to 60 percent of all pork and grapefruit. Thus Japan is, by a wide margin, the single largest recipient of American agricultural exports, including tobacco. So if American leaders are going to play with the dollar, they should do so against the currencies of Canada, Brazil, Australia, Thailand, and the other countries whose farmers are in competition with theirs to sell into the Japanese market. That is the way to make the prices of American farm products more attractive to Japanese consumers. Making the dollar cheaper against the yen is irrelevant. Our farmers are not competitive at any imaginable exchange rate.

Furthermore, the trade in goods does not rest upon a free-floating industrial base that can easily move itself around the world to accommodate FX fluctuations. Plants and factories are not the kinds of things you put on a trailer or steamer and move about. They tend to be fairly well bolted to the ground on which they stand. You can close them down, of course, but you cannot set them running about the world like a pack of bloodhounds hot on the trail of sweet-scented exchange rates. Nor do these facilities exist in a vacuum. They have critical linkages with all sorts of industrial infrastructure—suppliers, distributors, logistics networks, academic researchers, labor pools, and the like.

Money slips across borders in the blink of an electronic eye. Infrastructure cannot. The weight of historical evidence shows that most producers will try to sit out unfavorable FX movements where they are rather than starting from scratch in a new location to build up whole new infrastructural networks. Even if they were tempted to do otherwise, the time scale is off. By the time they get their new networks in place, the FX rates may have shifted again.

Even if they have, it will make little difference to the Japanese companies Americans are most worried about. Remember, only twenty Japanese firms account for 50 percent of all exports to the United States; the top fifty firms account for 75 percent. We know these companies. I have personally worked with many of them. They are, for the most part, currency neutral. They have slashed costs, moved production to the NIEs, and mastered *zaitech* (financial engineering). By becoming established insiders in their key foreign markets, they have matched the currencies of revenues and costs. In dozens of ways they have insulated themselves against FX fluctuations. The proof is that they have absorbed a halving of the dollar/yen rate during the past decade with no loss of competitive effectiveness. They are structured to make money even if the dollar goes lower. And if all attempts to neutralize the effects of the declining dollar were to fail, they can still use the strong yen to acquire dollar-based assets, including American competitors. Currency fluctuations only widen strategic options. They do not kill alert corporations fully versed in the ILE.

International competitiveness should be increased through improved productivity and quality, not through artificial currency manipulations. Trying to play the FX game against the statistical and political problems is not only wrong, but very damaging long term. Such game-playing will cost the United States a significant chunk of its industrial base and at least a generation of infrastructure, which is now gone and will not easily come back. Artificially expensive dollars during the early Reagan years forced quite a few American companies to seek offshore production. Artificially cheaper dollars have not pulled them back home but rather have made the *United States* itself inexpensive for foreigners to buy. FX should not be part of the industrial policy to give industry an easy time to rake in short-term profit, or reason to cry for lack of competitiveness. This is one refuge for scoundrels that should be closed down for good.

The Greenbacks Empire

A formal policy of keeping the dollar weak makes even less sense when you consider that, in currency-related terms, the United

States enjoys a unique position in the world. Because most of its trade transactions are dollar-based, it has in effect extended its domestic economy across national borders, creating in the process a huge "greenbacks empire." For Americans, it makes little ultimate difference to the national indebtedness whether they buy oranges from California or TV sets from Taiwan. Both amount to much the same thing. Americans in New York don't worry about running up a trade deficit with California. They don't need to worry about Taiwan either.

The U.S. dollar is the internationally accepted currency of trade settlement. In fact, it is virtually the only currency the United States uses to settle external trade. That means other countries have to earn and save dollars one way or another. They have to maintain these dollar-based reserves against the demands they face to pay for various imports. If they run out of dollars and cannot borrow them somewhere, they cannot purchase the critical resources they need or the luxuries they want. But this does not apply to the United States itself. It has—or can print—all the dollars it wants. To America's trading partners, this state of affairs feels like being swallowed up into a single, immense greenbacks empire—which is, in currency terms, merely an extension of the U. S. domestic economy. Simply stated, the United States has no *foreign* trade. There are plenty of reasons to worry about the health of a purely domestic economy, but statistical trade balances are not among them.

For the Japanese, the dollars earned by exporting goods to the United States are less like money to be put in the bank than a promissory note to buy American goods in the future. The Japanese cannot use the dollars at home. They are useless to them—unless they are able to return them to the United States and buy things. On the way back, however, they may well make a detour through the Middle East where the Japanese need them to pay for oil. Or they may go back home via the London market. Whatever route they take, the point is that they do not stay in Japan. Sooner or later, they have to be recycled through the domestic American economy.

If you buy a Sony Walkman in New York, you pay in dollars. Government statistics add the value of your purchase to the total of Japanese imports. It becomes part of the much-feared, but illusory, trade deficit. Why should that be so? Why should those dollars not be treated as being as much a continuing part of the expanded domestic economy, the greenbacks economy, as the dollars you spend in the shop next door for your California oranges? When those dollars get used again, they will be used to buy American goods. What's the difference? Many Japanese would like to be able to treat the yen this way, to deal with all other nations in yen. They would gladly trade places with the United States. This is not possible right now. But if the dollar continues to decline for the wrong and artificial reasons reflecting erroneous political and macroeconomic perceptions, America's trading partners will stop accepting dollars for their goods and services sold to the Americans. At that point, America becomes a Brazil. Why should the United States give up unnecessarily such an advantage it enjoys now?

With so many dollars in the hands of other countries, is the United States vulnerable should circumstances prompt these investors to unload? As discussed in chapter 9, if the American economy really does go sour, all smart money will flee—American money too. When Houston's oil-based economy went into a steep decline a few years back, it was not just the foreigners who pulled out. Americans did too, and just as fast. Money is money. It's the most purely rational thing there is. Foreign capital is in the United States because it is attractive for capital to be here. When that stops being the case, it will go away in a hurry. Yes, that will be a bad time for the United States—but not because the money goes. That's turning the logic wrong way around. Capital flight is only a symptom. Our interest is to keep America strong and attractive, not to raise unnecessary tensions around trade and currency and make currency and stock traders excessively nervous.

Borderless economy complicates the situation for those who believe in only time-honored, statistics-based, bilateral macroeconomic pictures. But it offers enormous opportunities to those who can crisscross the boundaries in search of better profits. We are finally living in a world where money, securities, services, options, futures, information and patents, software and hardware, companies and know-how, assets and memberships, paintings and brands are all traded without national sentiments across traditional borders.

11

Development in a
Borderless World

The globalization of consumer tastes and its effects on fixed costs, the rapid dispersion of technology, the explosive growth of the FX empire—in short, the cumulative, relentless flow of information around the globe—has taken years to alter the landscape long familiar to corporate strategists. But it has done its work well. Today if you look closely at the world Triad companies inhabit, national borders have effectively disappeared and, along with them, the economic logic that made them useful lines of demarcation in the first place. Not everyone, however, has noticed.

The Resource Illusion

In some parts of the world, national borders seem as intact as ever, impervious to the worldwide flow of information. This faulty vision is not accidental. It is the predictable result, most common today in such developing countries as Brazil, Chile or Indonesia, of a refusal or an inability to acknowledge that the economic logic of an earlier age no longer applies. During the many years it was in force, that logic—the belief that an ample stock of natural resources was what made a country rich and its products competitive—served as a powerful support for the idea of economic nationalism. If these resources were the primary source of national wealth, then foreign companies or countries that wanted access to them were, at best, tolerated intruders and, at worst, callous exploiters to be kept at bay by every available means.

If you think you have a single, limited pot of gold to defend, then you defend it as best you can. If you absolutely must sell some of it in order to have money enough to buy food or build shelter, then you do so—but with no love lost for the buyer. There is no welcome mat by the door. In fact, you keep the door triple-locked and hang a big "Go Away" sign on it that can be read from a great distance. Not surprisingly, you resent the circumstance that drives you to open your nation at all. You are protectionist in the most fundamental sense. You do not want entangling economic relationships. You do not want partnerships. You do not want to be part of any larger web of trade or exchange. What you want is to be left alone with your pot of gold.

Not all developing nations and NIEs adopt so defensive a posture, even those that are resource poor. In Taiwan there is understandably a strong upwelling of nationalism in the political arena, but not in industry. Leading South Korean companies participate actively and successfully in the global arena. Joint ventures and licensing arrangements flourish. In Hong Kong there is no economic nationalism, no reluctance to play a major role in the international flow of goods and services. The same is true of Singapore and increasingly of Thailand. Each of these is a healthy, vibrant economy. None is free of problems but all can boast of impressive economic performance and the rising standards of living that go along with it. But there is no boasting in Brazil. Unbelievable natural riches have not produced national wealth. In fact, they have gotten in the way.

The murderous effects of this resource illusion can, perhaps, best be seen in the case of Malaysia, which had suffered grievously from the British heritage of preserving the estate and mining sectors and underdeveloping the manufacturing sector so as not to compete with British imports. But it finally managed to shake the problem off. Malaysia is rich in resources. It enjoys every kind of blessing from the sun and the soil. It has oil, gas, copper, tin, palm oil, rubber, lumber, and much else besides. So until eight or so years ago, its storehouse of natural wealth chained it to a primary commodity-based economy, which proved volatile. The people had become lazy and complacent because they took all this natural richness for granted. Here and there strident back-to-the-soil nationalist movements took root. They tried to solve everything with Malays only, not counting for possible assistance from foreigners and their minority Chinese and Indian talents.

But Prime Minister Datuk Seri Mahathir told them that that was a dead-end course. "Look East" was his slogan, and he persuaded his people to learn from the work ethics of Japan, South Korea, Taiwan, and so on. Because these other countries did not enjoy anything like the resource base of Malaysia, they had had to find other ways to ensure the well-being of their people. Being resource poor, they had not had the occasion to fall into the resource illusion. And their experience showed it up for what it really was: a self-defeating excuse for not figuring out how to become a healthy part of the ILE.

There was considerable resistance to this "Look East" program—much of it from government bureaucrats who often held down two or three positions and rarely performed any of them. Now they had to punch in on a time clock each morning at 9:00 A.M. They didn't like that, but the change was essential. The Malasyian economy in general was sluggish, heading toward joining the league of debtor nations, but the government sector was flourishing. It was the country's only growth industry. Foreign investment was looked on with great suspicion. Just another attempt, most Malays thought, to steal their resources and exploit their people. All that has turned around. In 1988, for the first time in history, Malaysia's manufacturing exports surpassed those of primary commodities. Today, in fact, Malaysia is the largest exporter of semiconductor chips in the world, even larger than Japan in quantity terms. More industrial goods are exported than primary commodities now.

Malaysia is the happy exception that proves the unhappy rule. Most resource-rich countries have a provider's mentality. They still believe they can make it on their own and that the best thing they can do for their own development is lock the door as tightly as possible against the exploiters of the world. Even such advanced countries as Australia and Canada often fall into this dilemma. They think because they are resource rich they can live on their own resources, dipping leisurely into their pot of gold at need. But it doesn't work that way. Unless they are the sole source of some absolutely critical material, the resources on which they count can be easily arbitraged. They have become commodities. When no value is added, none can be collected. If the market for what they produce is healthy, the economy is okay. If it is not, the economy is in deep trouble—and there's nothing they can do about it. No real planning is possible because their critical markets are dependent on demand in the developed economies, which is extremely volatile and has a chronic tendency to slip into a situation of excess supply. No matter how rich they think they are, countries with a provider's mentality are at the mercy of these external fits and starts. They cannot really plan their own development.

It does not have to be this way. The island of Jamaica produces Blue Mountain coffee, which sells in Japan for four times the price of Brazilian coffee. Is it four times better? Probably not. Blind taste tests show little difference. What is different, however, is the clever and determined branding of the coffee—in other words, the managed effort to add value. This is no different from the value added by such fashion houses as Yves St. Laurent or Givenchy to products like neckties, which are probably made of the same material and with the same quality as other good neckties but cost five or six times as much. Agricultural products can be branded too. *Koshihikari* rice, which is produced in Niigata Prefecture, is 30 percent more expensive than normal rice. Kobe beef, Japan's finest, is two to three times more expensive than any other kind of Japanese-produced beef, which is two to three times again more expensive than beef from the United States or Australia. It is, indeed, very good. But branding creates this large margin of value.

When a country suffers from a provider's mentality, however, it does not think in terms of value-added. It thinks in terms of tons and bushels, of undifferentiated commodities. You grow it or pick it or mine it or collect it and then you cart it away. And in doing so, you leave an immense amount of money in the soil. You turn your back and walk away from the opportunity to add value. Just go to your local store. Sunkist oranges are more expensive than no-brand oranges; Indian River grapefruits more expensive than no-brand grapefruits. But if you are able to think only in terms of tons of citrus products, then you never make the effort to capture this marginal value.

Worse, you become increasingly isolationist. You reject out of hand the active participation in the global economy that can get you started on the road to healthy development. In your mind, every ton that leaves your shores represents the loss of a precious natural resource. You sell it because you have to, but you resent the necessity and the buyer. Because you've done nothing to add value, you get very little back from the industry chain into which your product moves. At the same time, of course, you have been getting yourself in debt with foreign banks. When the loans come due and the demands for repayment become more and more insistent, you turn further away from the rest of the world. But not without complaining loudly and bitterly in every public forum open to you about the rapacious greed of foreign exploiters who have stolen your resources for a pittance and have beggared you by lending you money.

Bitter experience shows that this is a great way to go nowhere. To develop economically, you must find ways to add value. To do that, you must understand customers well enough to figure out how best to differentiate your products. You must know, for example, that Americans prefer their beef lean but the Japanese like it well marbled. But unless you participate actively in the marketplace, you will have no way of finding this out. And once you are in the marketplace, you can begin to move into different parts of the industry chain. Someone else used to do the shipping for you, but you can take over the shipping yourself. This adds value. You also learn more about the industry and so can take on yet other activities. But to get this virtuous cycle started, you cannot be isolationist. You have to be willing to make connection with the ILE. Solutions are within the marketplace, not in a rather inexperienced government, a controlled economy, or depressed consumption and tariffs on imports.

Wealth is created, or can be found, in the marketplace or the ILE, not in the soil per se. This is the major paradigm shift that has occurred during the past decade. The two energy crises have given everyone the contrary impression. That is why it is taking so much time for most countries to recognize the emergence of the ILE as the creator of wealth. The reason: Any extended exposure to the global marketplace is a threat to well-entrenched bureaucracies at home, which live by the time-honored law of serving their own interests first. You wrap yourself in the flag of defiant nationalism and then proceed to starve a little more, fall a little farther behind, every year.

Years ago, when people were relatively misinformed, or uneducated, opening your economy meant falling prey to the exploitative multinational enterprise (MNE). That was the vision of things that held from the days of the East India Company though the MNEs of the 1960s. In today's economy, thanks to the freer flow of information, customers know better. They choose. And their decisions are a lot better than those of governments. For the governments to choose a handful of companies and give exclusive licenses to them to produce or sell in the local economy, they have to deny their own people access to the best and cheapest products. MNEs will exploit these opportunities when given so privileged a position. However, if the market is basically open, then even incumbent MNEs must always be on their toes.

A closed economy does not encourage the innovation, productivity, and improvement necessary to win in the Triad market. In Brazil, car and motorbike companies cannot import components easily, so they cannot produce products that are competitive in developed economies. For domestic markets this is acceptable, but it is not acceptable for exporting. By contrast, both Taiwan and South Korea allow their companies to import critical components from Japan and elsewhere. This is why these countries can produce goods that are competitive in the United States and Europe.

Such a policy allowed Taiwan to generate over a $10 billion trade surplus annually with the United States, which can more than compensate for its $5 billion deficit with Japan. Taiwan, through its close linkage with the ILE, has stored up $80 billion in foreign reserves, second only to Japan. Brazil and other resource-rich nations are still running their economies down debt's death spiral. Only a decade ago most of these economies were at par at $1,500 per capita GNP. Taiwan now is a $7,000 per capita GNP economy, while Brazil remains essentially where it was ten years ago.

Some argue that this is a small price to pay for independence. Unpleasant, surely, but necessary. Outsiders might question the trade-off between economic well-being and self-righteous assertions of autonomy, but what do they know? This is a value judgment, and you have made the one that best suits your people, your culture, your traditions. Moreover, if the independence of those complaining outsiders were threatened, they would quickly sing a different tune. Just look at the protectionist sentiments bubbling beneath the surface of the major industrial democracies. It is all a question of choice and degree. There are no absolutes. If you think it best to keep the door shut, who is to say you're wrong? Who is to say you put too high a value on independence? Closed doors give regulatory bureaucrats both authority and a source of corruption.

This is the kind of nationalistic argument that gets votes where voting is still permitted. But it is deeply flawed. There is, for example, never a referendum question on the ballot to determine a people's willingness to remain impoverished. Such niceties of democratic process aside, it is flawed because the outcome it seeks has become impossible in any civilized country. Crazed dictators can effectively seal borders shut, insulate their people from the rest of the world, and oppress them in the name of this or that ideological goal.

But in anything resembling the civilized world, there will be segments of the population that do participate, one way or another, in the larger global economy. In Brazil, Mexico, Argentina, and other high-inflation debtor nations, for example, the rich hedge against rampant domestic inflation by importing dollars— or at least linking their assets to dollars—like crazy. So for the government to keep the rest of its people cut off from that larger economy is to permit, even encourage, the country to become even further divided against itself internally. This is a slow form of national suicide.

This isolation can be accomplished more or less. You can lower the voting age to sixteen, as in Brazil. You can make sure that a growing percentage of your people cannot read or write. You can whip up nationalist passions and stage-manage protectionist rallies, bonfires and all. What you cannot do, however, is keep the social fabric of your nation whole or provide a better life for the majority of your people. If you want to do that, you have to create sustained economic growth. And in the late twentieth century that means becoming a part, an active part, of the borderless world. It means giving up the resource illusion and figuring out ways to add value. It means allowing the best and most sincere foreign companies to operate on your soil and to import whatever they need in order for the products they make to be globally competitive. It means spending money to explore and develop external markets. (The Japanese, for example, spend nearly a quarter of their total revenues from export in the marketplace, for example, to understand customers and to develop brands and channels of distribution.)

In an interlinked economy, even a depressed economy becomes

attractive. High unemployment is a welcome sign for an investor looking for a new plant location. Italy and the United Kingdom, once feared to be bankrupt, recovered because that state of affairs made them attractive to others. The connection of their economies with the European Community and the rest of the world saved them. In an interlinked economy there will be no absolute losers and winners. The all-too-familiar debt spiral of developing nations results from the old—and completely wrong—"nationalistic" model of where such an economy should draw its borders. The worse their economies become, the more their governments adopt isolationist, protectionist policies. This only makes the people's lives worse and worse.

How do these governments usually respond to such arguments? We cannot link up like that, they say. We are too small, too vulnerable. Our domestic economy is neither big nor healthy enough to give us any leverage in the outside world. If we did unlock the door, foreigners would pour in, snap up the resources we do have, take over everything else, sit themselves down by our fireside, and run things in their own interest. Or imports will soar and take our jobs away. We would become servants or worse in our own homes. We are not yet strong enough to prevent it if the door is unlocked. So we will keep it as tightly closed as ever. But Singapore, Hong Kong, Taiwan, and Switzerland do not exactly have large world-class domestic economies or immensely rich stores of natural resources. Resources in Brazil and Indonesia are at least several orders of magnitude greater than any of these. What the other nations do have, however, is the determination to succeed in the global marketplace. They have learned to live with the door unlocked.

It is all a question of what people believe—and of what their governments tell them. In Japan the "textbook" children learn from starts with the clear and explicit notion that the country is poor. It has no natural resources. It has to import much of what it needs to survive and to export enough to pay for all that. Adding value provides the margin that enables the Japanese to buy the food that is needed. Otherwise they starve. They must be a part of the global economy. There is no choice. In Brazil the "textbook" begins with the notion that the people are rich, unbelievably rich, blessed with every natural resource they might ever need. Well, we have seen where this kind of teaching leads.

Last year, during a visit I made to Brazil, one of the country's leading economists told me a story that had been making the rounds of his professional colleagues. An Argentinian came to Brazil, noted its rich natural abundance, and went back home to complain to God about the unfairness of it all. We're neighbors, he pointed out, and You've given them everything and us nothing. Don't worry, came the divine reply. I've given them Brazilians as well. A week or so later, when I visited Venezuela, a local entrepreneur told me the same story—only this time it was about a Colombian visiting Venezuela. In few countries where I have visited do people talk proudly about their government. Most of them think theirs is corrupt and restrictive.

There are no excuses for this. Size is no obstacle to economic development. Extent of domestic market is no obstacle. Lack of resources is no obstacle. Abundance of resources, properly managed, is no obstacle. What gets in the way of economic development is the illusion that effort is irrelevant and that participation in the borderless and interlinked economy is unimportant. It is a question of ambition, willpower, and management skill. Chanting "Yanqui go home" or issuing blunt warnings about the "yellow peril" may go down well with the public and keep a bankrupt bureaucracy in power. Virulent nationalism can hide a multitude of sins. But it cannot fuel growth or provide a better way of life. After a while it may not even be reversible. If you keep telling people the big lie long enough, they will start to believe it. If what they read in the papers and see on television every day reinforces the message, they will believe it. If all they are exposed to is a concerted effort to blame other countries for local problems, they will believe it. If they are told time and again that protectionism is the only safe course, they will believe it. And if all this goes on long enough, there may be no return. Or at least the road back will be a long one.

The End of National Interest

In the borderless world, it is harder every day to see where traditional national interests lie. Look, for a moment, at the Research Triangle in North Carolina. During the past two years, more than one-third of all the investments coming into the triangle have come from Japan. With whom or what does the triangle compete for such funds? Certainly not other countries. It is areas like Route 128 outside Boston or the Silicon Valley in California. The real battle, if battle there is, lies between regions, not countries.

If you are concerned about developing the economic base in Southern California, do you look to Washington? No. You get on a plane to Asia. You welcome the Asian investment that is flowing into your companies and your real estate. Asian interest in California used to be centered farther north, in San Francisco. Over the years, however, that city has taken such a conservative attitude toward development that it has driven trans-Pacific attention south toward Los Angeles or Orange County. This is not even a battle of regions—the competition here is between cities.

As the borderless and interlinked economy develops, regional- and city-level interests come more and more into play. In fact, informal pairings of cities—not the "sister city" hoopla of boosterism-minded chambers of commerce—have taken on greater importance. Hong Kong capital, controlled by those fearful of the looming 1997 reversion to Chinese control, has been moving quickly into Toronto. Many thousands of Hong Kong people have already moved, registered, bought real estate, or bought businesses there. Toronto is booming with Hong Kong money. This is so, in part, because Canada is one of only two nations (the other is Australia) that offer Hong Kong nationals the possibility of holding double passports—provided, of course, that they bring in a certain amount of foreign capital. Toronto appeals because of its long-established Chinese-speaking community and the infrastructure that has built up around it. More recently, money from Hong Kong and elsewhere in Asia has been flowing into

Vancouver as well. And 90 percent of net capital investment in the Gold Coast of Australia comes from Japan.

This kind of checkerboard of international investment has become common. Japanese money, for example, has not gone everywhere in Europe. Half of it goes to the United Kingdom and most of that to Wales, especially South Wales. Fifteen years of development have created a high-quality infrastructure of component suppliers, not very different from home. On the continent, the Japanese have paid special attention to Alsace-Lorraine, which is centrally located and very hospitable to foreign investment. In Asia, Hong Kong and Taiwan money goes to selected areas in China; Japanese money to certain areas in Malaysia, such as Selangor, Johore, and Penang. German money is gradually shifting to the southern states of Baden-Württemberg and Bayern, and Hamburg suffers. Northern European capital is pouring into southern Spain around Barcelona.

The linkages vary but the pattern is clear: The global economy follows its own logic and develops its own webs of interest, which rarely duplicate the historical borders between nations. As a result, national interest as an economic, as opposed to a political, reality has lost much of its meaning. And as information about products and services becomes more universally available, consumers everywhere will be able to make better-informed choices about what they want. It will matter less and less where it all comes from. Governments—and the national boundaries they represent—become invisible in this kind of search. They have no direct role to play. There is no call for them to continue to pick and choose which products can be produced or sold or to decide which are good and which bad. The economic interests to be served are those of individual consumers. Governments do not need to insulate or protect them from the offerings of multinational companies. Consumers can make their own choices. And they do.

Certainly, difficulties remain. The old approach—government must protect the people from exploitation—dies hard. In India, for example, domestic automobiles are not very good. The government has determined what this "national car" should be and has stuck with one model for more than thirty years. Yes, it's cheap, but it is such an old and miserable design that it runs poorly and is expensive to maintain. In Malaysia, efforts to impose national cars now meet with resentment and protest from a well-informed public. The government can still put a hefty surcharge on imports, but it can be in the range of only 30 percent or so, not the 100 or 200 percent like India. In time, even that 30 percent will be hard to maintain. Better information makes for better choices. Venezuela is also rapidly changing its isolationist policies and lowering tariffs to the 50 percent range for automobiles and other amenities.

Japan has moved far along this path, but it still has a way to go. The government continues to claim, for example, that Japanese blood is different enough from North American and European blood that all drugs approved elsewhere in the Triad must go through five years of clinical tests to be reapproved in Japan. This is for the good of the people, they say. This is to protect them from drugs like thalidomide that wrecked such havoc elsewhere. But it is really only a way to protect their own turf and their own power. In fact, when Japanese consumers sued the government for having approved drugs that proved to have harmful side effects, the powers-that-be claimed that they were not legally responsible. The companies were at fault. Everyone in Japan now sees that the government was trying to have it both ways—in its own interest, not that of its people. This cannot last much longer. The people have seen through it.

In Hong Kong, by contrast, the colonial government takes a very different, "free port" approach. With this approach, Hong Kong has achieved a $10,000 per capita GNP economy, the same level as Her Majesty's homeland. Hong Kong's approach has some merit in today's world. For example, if a drug has been approved by a responsible government elsewhere, it can be sold in Hong Kong. If it causes harm, the government is not at fault and cannot be sued. You were just unlucky. If there is to be legal action, it must be aimed at the companies, not the government.

But such action is rare. The people understand that they make choices and must accept the consequences. There are no perfect guarantees. If you choose to live in a dangerous area, you accept the risk that you may get mugged or shot down in the street. This is a very different mind-set from the one in Japan, where people feel they should be able to blame the government for any breakdown in their security. And it is still different from the United States, where litigation is the national pastime.

A Pluralism of Values

More than anything else, the burgeoning flow of information directly to consumers is eroding the ability of governments to pretend that their national economic interests are synonymous with those of their people. The better informed people are, the more they will want to make their own choices and the less those choices will square with the boundary lines drawn years ago on maps. This is especially true at a time when the changing nature of international business itself makes it ever more difficult to attach meaningful national labels to specific products.

This is just another way of describing the borderless world. But it has an important—and often overlooked—corollary: This flow of information is not really creating anything new. It is not segmenting consumer taste or choice. Instead, it is making it possible, at last, for the many variations in taste around the world to find concrete expression. As the boundary lines on maps fade, the underlying clusters of value and preference become increasingly visible.

People vary in how they want to live. There is no universal style, nor even a style that holds firmly at the national level. We all know this. What has changed in the past few years is the ability of the interlinked economy to accommodate that variation and that multiplicity of styles. By definition, such an economy is pluralist. Many countries, however, are at war with pluralism.

Some suffer from the resource illusion and impose nationwide choices as the price of holding the rest of the world at bay. Others, including those governed by communist regimes, are ideologically committed to the notion that each country should have a single value system—and that, defined by the party. Their failure to date is the result of a deeply mistaken fundamental assumption. They try to plan, but they cannot plan ahead with any certainty.

In today's world, however, like Feigenbaum's chaos, nothing can be predicted with certainty if the phenomenon is caused by so many variables. This is true even in a small economy. But it is absolutely the case in the borderless world, in which any small movement in any part of the ILE can trigger a crash or surge in FX across all borders and many other serious side effects. We can increase our ability to respond to volatility and even chaos, but we cannot with any certainty *plan* our economy, as Karl Marx and the other early pioneers of communism hoped we could. The verdict of history is already in: Communist doctrine cannot survive in an interlinked economy—unless, of course, the entire world suddenly decides to obey the commands and edicts of a single dictator.

Our challenge is to help the nations that have long been economically shielded from—but gradually connected through information flows with—the ILE to establish linkages with our economies at a pace that is manageable by their own governments. An overly rapid liberalization of their economies—for example, too quick an effort to link them with the already interlinked Western economy—will tear their social fabric. The result of that wrenching change will not please anybody, including the Western nations that are currently toasting their victory in the Cold War.

Still other nations, such as Japan, have not entirely shed their nineteenth-century belief that development is best and most efficiently accomplished under the stern, guiding hand of a government that tells the people what is good for them (and that does not give them enough freedom of choice for them to think otherwise). Japan, South Korea, and Taiwan have a long way to go to liberate their people from the central power of government or of the leading party. Their success to date is because of their governments. No question about it. But their future agonies will also be the result of their governments. In these countries real pluralistic choice in political ideologies within a democratic and capitalistic regime is yet to come.

The situation in Japan is becoming critical. Japan has climbed up from the ashes of World War II and a gross national product of about $300 per capita to reach the heavyweight class among industrialized nations. Now this remarkable economic growth seems to be coming to an end because the government has not converted itself into a modern, democratic, "developed nation" mode of operation.

Until 1980, when Japan joined the $10,000 per capita GNP club of the advanced countries, it was a model developing nation. The government built ports, bridges, highways, schools, hospitals, and railways. When industries were weak, it protected them. It gave the Japanese people a value system, based on the rationalization that given the country's lack of natural resources, they must work hard to create value through exports and buy food with the surplus. Individual prosperity inevitably would result.

That system has worked. The standard of living has increased steadily over the past forty years; more than 90 percent of the people consider themselves middle class and reasonably happy about their life.

The people have given their leading and only credible political party, the Liberal Democratic Party, clear and uninterrupted power for almost forty years. The LDP won by a landslide in the election in July 1986. But less than two years later the LDP started to crumble, and dissent rose to unprecedented heights.

The symptoms all point to one thing: Japan does not have a modern government. Its government still wants to sit in the driver's seat, step on the gas, apply the brakes and steer, with 120 million people in the backseat. Yet in a modern system, the government's role is to give the people as much choice as possible and to keep them well informed so they are capable of making a choice. It also allows people to buy the best and the cheapest goods from anywhere in the world.

The Japanese government doesn't allow this. The Ministry of Agriculture and Fishery actually is a ministry for farmers and fishermen instead of a ministry of provisions. The Ministry of Health and Welfare is a ministry of doctors and pharmaceutical companies rather than an organization dedicated to protecting the health of the people. The Ministry of Education is nothing but a cartel for licensed teachers, and certainly does not act on behalf of students. The Ministry of Construction spreads concrete throughout the country and boasts in international conferences that Japan's paved roadway per capita is the longest in the world, but it seldom thinks of the poor commuters who spend so much time sitting in traffic. The Ministry of Transportation serves the industry, certainly not the passengers who must pay extraordinarily high prices.

And the Ministry of Foreign Affairs works for itself, supporting Japanese diplomats who sprinkle abundant aid money around the world to ensure that their seat at the dinner table is next to the host's. This ministry has done nothing to correct the misunderstandings and misperceptions that are at the root of Japan's deteriorating image. Instead, it seems to be using foreign pressure (particularly that of the United States) and even the trade conflict to expand its sphere of influence vis-à-vis other ministries.

All this illustrates that Japanese ministries still have a "provider" mentality; they do not serve the people, and particularly not consumers. They serve themselves, the industries, and the special-interest groups. The rest of the world accepted such methods when Japan was developing. Japanese people also put up with it because the government provided job stability and growing paychecks.

Japan is a bureaucratic country, not a political one. The Diet plays a minor role compared with the powerful bureaucratic system. Most bills are drafted by bureaucrats, not politicians. The Diet doesn't normally even debate bills, because the opposition parties are so strongly opposed to whatever the LDP does that it would be a waste of time. So most bills are passed without full discussion; particularly difficult bills are passed in the absence of the opposition parties.

A recent example is the 3 percent consumption tax on all commercial activities. This makes enormous sense in Japan, where direct tax accounts for more than 70 percent of revenues and the capture rate of direct tax is so unfair. If you are a salaried person, Amen! One hundred percent captured. If you are a retailer, 50 percent, and a farmer, 30 percent. To correct this inequality of collection, most people would have favored an indirect tax, such as a consumption tax. But the bill was passed without debate in the Diet, in the absence of the opposition. As a result, the Japanese people didn't know what to expect when the new law was introduced on April 1, 1989. They were frustrated by the longer lines at the cashier and the small coins given as change. All of a sudden prices were no longer in denominations of 100 or 200. They were 103 or 206. Pockets exploded with one-yen aluminum coins.

While people were jingling their change, the LDP politicians were caught in scandals. Money, such as in Recruit's political donations, and women, as in the cases of Prime Minister Sousuke Uno and Secretary General Tokuo Yamashita, seldom have caused political scandals in Japan. But in an information-dominated era, we cannot contain the Gary Hart syndrome in the United States alone. What is newsworthy spreads across the ILE. Whereas most men were a bit ambivalent about the sex scandals (though they were furious about Recruit), women were upset about both and surged to the polls. In the 1989 Upper House and Tokyo metropolitan congressional elections, in which the Socialist Party won a runaway victory, 60 percent of eligible women voted, as opposed to the usual 40 percent. It is difficult to analyze how much of their anger was due to Recruit, the sex scandals, or the one-yen coins in their purses, but they obviously were voting to punish the LDP.

Taken by surprise, the Socialist Party is busy changing its

doctrines. It's now okay, they say, to deal with the United States, along with the Soviet Union. Nuclear power plants are acceptable. The U.S.–Japan Security Treaty can continue, sort of. And so on. They are even trying to change their own party's name, to diffuse the bad image coming from the falling of socialist countries.

Against the rapid cosmetic overhaul of the Socialist Party, the LDP has been paralyzed. Now is the time to reform the government from a provider, developing-country vanguard role to that of a modern, industrialized nation in which consumers have the ultimate choice. If the LDP, as currently composed, can't make the transformation, then it should split into two parties. One party could stand for consumer interests, small government, free trade, and globalism to put Japan clearly among the most developed and open countries in the ILE. The other party could continue on the traditional LDP track, representing the manufacturers' preference for larger government, control, regulation and protectionism, and denying the entry into the ILE.

In Japan or elsewhere, the stark, unavoidable economic fact of life is that none of these denials of pluralism works any longer. The countries suffering from the resource illusion are bowed down with debt and falling way behind in development; the communist world is in chronic, probably terminal, economic disrepair; and the Japanese and their clones are profoundly dissatisfied with the whole structure and operation of their central government. No country represents a single value system, and no effort to pretend that it does—or to act as if it does—is both credible and effective.

In Japan, for example, Hokkaido may want to become the Switzerland of Asia and a hub for international air travel. Tokyo may want to go its own way. Osaka's interests may lie in becoming the capital of East Asia and not competing with Tokyo. The three cities of Tokyo, Osaka, and Nagoya and their satellites account for nearly 85 percent of the Japanese economy. They are doing fine, but the rest of the population has legitimate doubts about just how far the health of these cities has any spillover benefits for them. There is no coherent, one-dimensional Japanese value system any longer. Regions pull in different directions, and consumer preferences vary by individual all over the map. For example, the Kansai area, encompassing the three cities of Osaka, Kobe, and Kyoto, is a $500 billion economy. It it were a country, it would be ranked seventh in the world, after the United Kingdom but before Canada. It has 20 million people with very different tastes and value systems from those of Tokyoites. Japan can't be treated as a single economy with one cluster of people by any sensible marketing men and women.

The same, of course, is true elsewhere. The political boundaries of the United States do not encompass a single value system. In Eastern Europe, the evidence is irrefutable that consumers want to be part of the broader European economy. The drab theoretical uniformity of their failed economies has long since given way to countless experiments with one or another aspect of capitalism. The same is true in China, although the recent tragedies have set things back. But change will have to come—not least because per capita GNP in China still hovers at about $300 per year while the corresponding figure for Taiwan is $7,000 and the people have begun to find this out.

Myanmar (formerly Burma) and Thailand were at about the same stage of development twenty-five years ago. But Thailand has opened itself to the global economy and flourished while Myanmar has shut itself off and fallen backward. Its people have begun to discover what has happened in Thailand and in the rest of the world. So they resist further stagnation—even as their government pursues it as a matter of policy. Their border with Thailand is defined by two narrow rivers, the Me Nam and the Thanlwin, and the long lines of river-crossing shoppers in Thailand from Myanmar are just another indication of consumers voting with their feet—and their pocketbooks—whenever they exercise freedom of choice. Likewise, the flood of Japanese at the duty-free shops in airports around the world is nothing but a badge of shame for their government, which does not give them the same privileges of choice at home.

Just follow the headlines in the newspapers: People every-where, sometimes at great personal risk, are making it clear that they want to participate in the global economy. They want to find expression for their diverse mix of tastes and preferences. What they do not want is for some central government to tell them which kinds of choices they have to make in the personal areas of their lives. Economically, what they—what we all—are after is a good life, a life in harmony with our own values, values themselves shaped by individual choice. The role of government is not to make these choices but to ensure that the people can and do. No system can provide a good life for its people that is not sensitive to, that does not develop out of, the irreducible fact of pluralism. And that is the fact on which the interlinked economy rests.

12

A Steady Hand

It is hard to let old beliefs go. They are familiar. We are comfortable with them and have spent years building systems and developing habits that depend on them. Like a man who has worn eyeglasses so long that he forgets he has them on, we forget that the world looks to us the way it does because we have become used to seeing it that way through a particular set of lenses. Today, however, we need new lenses. And we need to throw the old ones away.

We have to accept the fact that, for developing and developed economies alike, for Canada and Australia as well as for Brazil and the OPEC nations, natural resources are no longer the key to wealth. We have to accept that national borders have little to do any longer with the real flows of industrial activity. We have to accept that information and knowledge—a trained and literate population, not military hardware—are the real sources of strength. The better informed people are, the more they know what is going on elsewhere in the world, the more they will want for themselves all those things that make life pleasant and enjoyable. And the more they will want to make their own choices among them.

A Role for Government

Governments can, of course, try to deny these facts or to keep them from us. But such efforts work less and less well. Information spreads. The people know. In particular, they know that it is governments which either allow that information to reach them unimpeded or try to shut it out or control it. At the same time, they know that the capacity of those governments to generate wealth is no longer based on the richness of what lies on or under the soil or on their legal ability to tax or on their military ability to stake a claim to colonial dependencies. It is based instead on the hard and dedicated work of well-trained and well-educated people. And such people will, by definition, be knowledgeable about developments elsewhere in the interlinked economy.

Caught between these new realities, what can responsible governments do? The answer is simple: Educate their people and see to it that they have as much information—and as much choice—as possible. Any other course is, at best, a holding action. Worse, it is a holding action that cannot long be successful but that can easily alienate the people. If foreign companies want to set up factories or sell products in a country, governments should not stand in the way. These companies and their products do not represent the edge of exploitation. They represent the availability of greater choice and greater satisfaction.

In the interlinked economy, it does not matter who builds the factory or who owns the office building or whose money lies behind the shopping mall or whose equity makes the local operation possible. What matters is that the global corporations that, one way or another, do business within a set of political borders act as responsible corporate citizens. If they do, no matter what their home country, they will treat the people fairly, give them good work to do, and provide them with valuable products and services. If they do not, the people will neither work for them nor buy what they produce.

Today's global corporations are nationalityless, because consumers have become less nationalistic. True global corporations serve the interests of customers, not governments. They do not exploit local situations and then repatriate all the profits back home, leaving each local area the poorer for their having been there. They invest, they train, they pay taxes, they build up infrastructure, and they provide good value to customers in all the countries where they do business. This is not altruism on their part. Nor is it a calculated effort to win good press that will stop as soon as attention moves elsewhere. This is simply good—in fact, essential—business.

If governments need not be so fearful of these foreign-based companies that they erect barriers against them, that does not mean their obligations to their people have ended. They still have the responsibility, now more important than ever, of educating those people and of providing first-class infrastructure for the businesses that will employ them and provide them with goods and services. They must make their countries an attractive enough location for the global companies to want to do business and invest and pay taxes there. Even better, they should nurture their local companies to grow into the global arena. The medium-size city Hamamatsu in Japan has produced several global companies: Yamaha, Honda, Suzuki, Kawai, and Hamamatsu Photonics. If the city does not support them, those companies will look elsewhere.

Well-run multinationals no longer seek to exploit local resources, to strike private deals with governments for licenses to operate within their borders. What they come looking for now are good markets and good workers, and they bring, in exchange, not private deals for officials but the promise of a better life for the people. These are promises to which governments must be ready to respond. The fact that the companies are foreign simply does not matter or, if it does, it is an advantage, not a problem. It means that the host government need not provide them tax credits or subsidies or special support for R&D. It would, for example, be terribly expensive for the Gaullist French government to require that a purely French company develop all the top-of-the-line mainframe computers used in France. Why not let IBM or Fujitsu provide them? Why not give people the choice?

During the New Deal regulation of the financial markets in the United States, the dominant theory espoused by Felix Frankfurter and others was that markets worked best when investors could make informed choices. Before then, such choices had been hard to come by—at least for most people—because the information needed to make them had not been widely or evenly shared. The solution, then, was for government to "let in the light"—that is, to make sure the information provided was full, accurate, and generally available. "Letting in the light" is still the right course for government. Let the people have all the information they need to make prudent choices, and then give them the freedom to make them.

At the same time governments have to provide infrastructure, and that costs money. So they must tax the global companies that operate within their borders. But there are limits here too. The amount of tax assessed and the services provided in exchange for it is a scoreboard for how well the government is performing. If its needs are great, if it has not done enough to educate its own people, then it will have to tax more. If it does, then it will become a less attractive place for those companies to do business. If it is erratic in the demands it makes on them, they will stay away. Global companies have the right to make informed choices too.

Inevitably, as these patterns of choice make themselves felt, some nations will be more badly hurt than others. That is why, inevitably, there must be a supergovernmental body of some sort that can monitor such developments and cushion the worst of their effects. As long as the nations in question are making determined efforts to get themselves back into competitive shape, there is good reason to help them along. That is because, in an interlinked borderless economy, the old zero-sum logic does not hold. If South Korea prospers, there are greater opportunities for everyone else. If Thailand joins the $10,000 GNP per capita club, everyone benefits.

In today's world there is no such thing as a purely national economic interest. American and Japanese interests, for example, are spread out all over the world. An American's attractive home mortgage may be financed by the blood, sweat, and tears of Tokyo's sardine-packed commuters, who are willing to put up with the conservative legal and economic system that created their nation's shaky real estate boom. That is probably to the good, because changing the laws or draining the rice paddies abruptly would likely cause a collapse of Tokyo's real estate prices. And that, in turn, would burst the Tokyo stock market bubble—and, along with it, the interlinked equity and real estate markets in the rest of the developed world.

Much the same is true of the U.S. government's budget deficit. If it were to disappear overnight, the sudden burst of strength in the dollar would distort capital flows all over the world. Money would flood into the United States to buy dollars or dollar-denominated paper. To slow down the capital drain, Japan and other nations would have to raise their interest rates by a significant amount. But if they did so, many thousands of the highly leveraged stock and real estate owners in Japan, who are used to living in a very-low-interest environment, would go bankrupt. The markets would crash, and the effects of that crash would instantaneously spread to the rest of the world. There is no immunity in an interlinked economy. This is the price we have to pay for having deregulated the financial and other markets. However, this does not argue for reregulation. Rather it demands an objective assessment of what we have created and what responsibilities we owe to each other. We need to understand the nature of the interlinked economy in an objective way, without any nationalistic overtones. We have to realize that we are in this *together*.

The economies of individual nations, such as the United States and Japan, are not firmly on the ground. They are like two planes aloft with the hydraulics of each pilot's levers linked partially to the flaps of the other plane. Unilateral actions are thus dangerous, perhaps fatal. Cooperation is essential, more so every day as the activities of global companies further spin the web of connected-ness. This is the question we should be debating in public fora and in the press. This is the fact of life with which we all have to learn to make a productive peace. But this is not what we most talk or yell about. What still grabs the headlines and dominates the legislative agenda is the perceived unfairness of trade and the arguments as to who is right.

We should face facts. For example, the American shipbuilding industry is in decline because it lost its American customers, notably the huge oil- and cargo-shipping companies. The reason why American users of large ships opted for Japanese ships is that they provided better value: They were cheaper and/or better. It is precisely for the same reason that Japanese shipyards lost their ground to the South Koreans. If the Koreans can produce ships to satisfy customer requirements better than anyone else in the world, that is where the demand will—and should—go. The only way for the Japanese shipyards to regain their superiority is through recovery of technological and cost leadership, not through trade negotiations.

When protests ring out over this loss of yet another American market, chances are the voices airing them are linked to minds that still believe there is something called "international competition" based on national flags. Surely a government can subsidize certain industries for a period of time. But such an action has to be supported by the taxpayers or by other industries or both. It does not come out of thin air. Either the industry or the company will lose its competitiveness.

If you look for an industry that has made its mark for a sustained period of time because of continuing government subsidies or guidance, you will look for a long time. Such industries often become docile because they lose touch with the competitive realities of the world. Government can stimulate, facilitate, and even foster the growth of certain industries. This is true of American venture capital and Japanese semiconductors and robots. But it would be naive to believe that Steve Jobs and Bill Gates have been the products of the American government.

Likewise, Koji Kobayashi and Tadahiro Sekimoto of NEC,

Genichi Kawakami of Yamaha, and Seiuzaemon Inaba of Fujitsu-Fanuc (a world leader in NC-robots) would laugh at the idea that they have achieved their place in the world thanks to the Japanese government.

Today if a corporation does not like its government, it can move its headquarters to other, more hospitable places. A number of preeminent Swedish companies (Novel and Tetrapak, for instance) are now based in Switzerland. Some Japanese companies are establishing R&D laboratories in the United States to take advantage of the flexible, creative minds of American engineers and scientists. Likewise, more than two thousand American companies have established manufacturing and service organizations in Japan to take advantage of a skilled, dedicated, and hardworking labor force that is still deeply loyal to the companies for which it works. It is true that they have taken themselves out of Uncle Sam's list of exporters from the United States, but they are prosperous in Japan under the American equity ownership.

When money, goods, people, information, and even companies crisscross national borders so freely, it makes no sense to talk of "American industrial competitiveness." The only thing that matters is that IBM competes with DEC and Fujitsu. But to maintain its competitiveness, IBM may have to buy memory chips from Hitachi, printers from Epson, software from Microsoft, and keyboards from Taiwan. Or it may choose to produce everything in-house, not because it wants to please Uncle Sam but because that is the best way to satisfy customers and beat DEC and NEC. In reality, however, IBM has traditionally produced products in all the key countries it serves.

Boeing has become the global champion of commercial aircraft, perhaps initially by leveraging Department of Defense money for military aircraft. But if that were the only reason for its success, why cannot other companies with defense contracts also build up a commercial aircraft business? Arguments about "Japan Inc." in the United States always fail to consider this. They miss the whole "blood, sweat, and tears" aspect of what companies have to do to become global competitors.

Toyota, Honda, and Nissan are often lumped together in

American and European minds as the "Japanese automobile industry under the auspices of MITI." But these companies succeeded because they fought against government interference. Until a little over a decade ago, MITI believed that the nine Japanese passenger-car companies could not survive in the world dominated by Detroit's Big Three. It tried to persuade them to merge to form a global-scale company. It tried to dissuade Honda from entering the market altogether because such a move would overcrowd an already fragmented industry. It was the individual companies' efforts to survive that made them successful, not the helping hands of MITI bureaucrats.

Even in the airline industry, where the influence of government has been strong due to old-fashioned concepts such as "national flag carriers," natural processes have a way of working out. If American airlines were permitted free access to domestic routes in Japan, they would not make any money if they failed to provide the quality of service that attracted Japanese passengers. And if they made no money, sooner or later they would withdraw. No protectionist barriers here, just the ability to satisfy customers, which is as it should be. I have argued many times in Japan that Japanese air space should be open to all airlines committed to serving the passengers in their best interest.

Governments should not be in the business of dictating choices to their people. Yes, they should provide guidance on issues of safety, acceptable minimum levels of service, and the like, and then they should stand back and let the people vote with their pocketbooks. If an American carrier provides the best air service in Japan, great. The Japanese are all the better for it. If an American bank provides the best consumer financial services in Japan, wonderful. As long as these companies treat their employees well and pay the proper taxes, why should the Japanese government care who owns their equity or where their headquarters are located? What possible difference does it make?

It is unwise for governments to get involved in the decision of who owns or should own a private enterprise. If the company does not serve the public well, if it scrimps on safety or ignores public health standards or treats employees illegally, it should be punished accordingly.

But if it is not very good at what it does, if it does not take great care with its people or its customers, they will leave it. There can be no presumption that a Japanese company would treat customers or employees any better than would a company based in the United States or France or the United Kingdom. It all depends on management. That, for example, is why Banyu, now majority owned by Merck, is performing much better than it did under Japanese ownership. At the time the acquisition produced much skepticism and anxiety among the Japanese who worked for Banyu. Today the results—and workers' attitudes—speak for themselves. And that too is exactly as it should be.

The role of government in a borderless world, then, is to represent and protect the interests of its people, not of its companies or its industries. It should let in the light and then allow its people to make their own choices. Anything less is to put the class and career interests of government bureaucrats ahead of those people they are sworn to serve.

Responsibilities of the Press

If the Rockefeller Group sells its assets to Mitsubishi Real Estate, that is because its manager wants to remain liquid and free up capital to do something else. Mitsubishi is probably the most conservative and hence attractive partner it could find in the world. Why should the press get excited about it, as if Japanese troops had invaded the heartland of America? The answer is simple: The press are still playing the old game of nationalism. They too need to be educated afresh in the facts of the ILE. They have lived too long agitating people with the paradigms of the Cold War and cannot write a story without a fictitious "enemy" in mind. Their model is always a James Bond story with a good guy and a bad guy.

American journalism in particular has become hysterical about Japan. *Newsweek* carried a cover story "Japan Invades Hollywood," with the Statue of Liberty clad in a kimono. The same issue, published in the Pacific, had the headline read "Japan Moves into Hollywood." Its Japanese-language edition containing the same article says "Sony Marches into Hollywood." This means that *Newsweek* understands the difference in the semantics between "invade" and "move into." And yet its choice of the former for the domestic American edition indicates that even this prestigious magazine, which aspires to be an opinion leader for global businesspeople, chooses to slant its semantics toward arousing ill-fated nationalism. When a group of Mitsubishi executives met with their counterparts at Daimler-Benz to talk about possible areas of collaboration, the same magazine carried an article entitled "A Courtship of Air Legends," and hinted at the shakehands of the Zeros and the Messerschmitts of the Second World War.

The Japanese press are no better. Several journals and TV stations called on me to write an article entitled "What's Wrong with Buying Rockefeller Center?" I, of course, knew better.

The American press made no noise when their corporations were buying up European companies in the 1960s and 1970s. Nor did they complain when wealthy Americans were buying up Paris apartments by the dozens when the French franc fell below 12 to the dollar in the mid-1980s or, more recently, when Ford bought Jaguar, GM bought Saab-Scania, and Campbell Soup bought Godiva chocolates. Of course, the Europeans were crying out then about "le defi americain." But American journalism, highly intellectual and creative as it is, still all too easily embraces a developing country's mentality when it comes to trade and asset sales. Memories are short. During the 1970s the press kept writing as if the United States would fall victim to Arab dollars and their buying up Manhattan and Beverly Hills. The money is still there. But nobody talks about it now.

Today's high-quality investments from overseas are like the immigrants in years past who helped build up America's economy and society. They are here to stay. They are willing to accept a lower return (compared with the return American money now demands), just as the immigrants were willing to work at a lower wage. And they free up the "native" investment dollars to more exciting and interesting instruments.

Most Japanese investments in the United States are in the form of these "immigrant dollars." They are in high-quality real estate, long-term government bonds, (low-interest rate) debt, and (at the most) the mezzanine portion of LBO funds. This investment of over $200 billion of fresh Japanese capital that accepts an "immigrant" status of low return has contributed to the stability of American financial markets, which, for their part, constantly seek high-risk/high-return opportunities.

Journalists and politicians, still bound by the old models of mercantilism and the Cold War, are slow to applaud these healthy developments. Instead they foster unnecessary tension. For, perhaps, the first time in modern history, the interdependence of national economies is creating not only security, but unprecedented prosperity. This should be the cause of celebration. Sadly, it is not. In its place what we find is a new—and unnecessary—wave of tension.

It's too bad these troubled and troubling voices are so loud. But most successful American and European companies in Japan hardly speak up. That's why unsuccessful businessmen in Washington and in Brussels excessively dominate air time. It's always possible to create a story that stirs up heated emotions by turning the failure of a small baseball bat company or chip producer, the arguable violation of ambiguous Cocom trade restrictions, or the mistranslation of a kitchen conversation into a vote-getting, newspaper-selling melodrama.

We all benefit from an era in which consumers are finally winning the right to choose—and have the information with which to choose intelligently. But these same consumers can rapidly become nationalistic voters if all they read and see and hear are stories of economic invasions or power plays. The benefits of this new era are real but fragile. The shadows of protectionism still lie close at hand. It does not take much to stir them up and set them to do mischief.

Perhaps as we move into the twenty-first century, we need a

supergovernment—maybe something like an extended European Community to encompass the Triad. Or maybe Japan and the United States will come up with a common economic framework and invite the Europeans and other nations to join. One way or another, however, we have to keep a growing skepticism from breaking the promise of the interlinked economy. No matter what doomsayers claim, we have a right to be optimistic that interdependence will provide a new means for assuring international security. The unarguable truth is that people have the right to live well and to choose the best and cheapest from anywhere in the world.

National Soil

A government's influence in these matters, however, extends farther than the reach of its explicit efforts to intervene in the activities of global corporations. The system of values and expectations that inevitably builds up around such formal interventions provides much of the soil in which those companies try to grow their businesses. As I argued in chapter 7, not every kind of plant grows well in the same patch of soil. And patches of soil can vary considerably in the kinds of growth they will support. These differences have consequences.

The United States, for example, is fertile ground for the start-up of small entrepreneurial companies. That is where the nation's economic dynamism rests. That is where most of its new jobs get produced. You have a great new idea, you define a niche you can serve, you get financing, you open your doors, you win customer approval, you take your company public and cash in through capital gains on the value you have created. That, in fact, is when the company probably has the highest value for you. Operations are just at the threshold of major capital investments. Market potential looks extremely bright. Reactions to your business idea are uniformly positive. So that's when it makes the best economic sense to sell the company and cash in on what you have created, a phenomenon known as the "American Dream."

If, however, you grow your company to five thousand or so employees, everything changes. You face a whole new set of problems with which, as an entrepreneur, you do not usually have any special expertise. Problems expand. Demands for performance become more insistent. The additional value the market will give you even for good performance goes down. Improvements now become incremental. You have to work harder for less, a phenomenon known as the "American Nightmare." Compensation, linked to these incremental improvements, grows more slowly. So the time to get out is early on when the getting is good. You can pocket your money and not have to be bothered with the less glamorous, day-to-day chores of actually running a steady-state company. You don't have to worry about the social or the environmental critics. You don't have to find ways to please the analysts who breathe ever more closely down your neck. You don't have to worry about the segment-wise disclosure and the state of things in five years. You are free—and rich.

When companies reach this kind of initial steady state, the leverage of individual decisions on market value plummets. Incremental choices produce, at best, incremental gains. To get the market interested again, you have to do something drastic: buy, sell, restructure. To get its attention, you have to do something discontinuous, something dramatic, something major. For the most part, however, we know that most real, lasting improvements come from the hard daily slog to do things better, to improve the accuracy of this system or that product, to reduce the life-cycle cost of the goods you provide to customers. So you are torn between doing what you think is right long term and what the market requires of you in this quarter and the next. Who needs that grief? Pocket your windfall and move on.

In Japan, by contrast, the national soil is much less nourishing for start-ups but much more so for established, steady-state companies. Once such a company is in existence, both managers and workers know that drastic, discontinuous changes are not really in the cards. There will be no binge of buying and selling. The company, for good or ill, is your world, and you have to make the best of it that you can. It is your community. You belong to it and will continue to belong to it for the rest of your working life. All you can do is try to make it better, to improve its products, to make incremental gains wherever possible.

Minolta's new Alpha 7000 is a single-lens reflex camera with an automatic focus. Customers complained that previous versions of automatic focus were fine unless the objects they were trying to photograph were moving. Then the images got blurred. In response, Minolta's engineers developed what was, in effect, a kind of mini–missile tracking system that can extrapolate the trajectory of a moving object, compute its new location, and refocus on that new spot within a hundredth of a second. Now, this technical capability exists in the United States too. It is embedded in any number of defense-related weapons systems. But put it or a version of it in a single-lens reflex camera for consumer use? Probably not. The returns will not be great enough. But for Minolta, which is married to the camera business, the situation is different. They have to make their cameras better any way they can. That is their business. And that will be their business tomorrow and the day after.

The national soil in the United States, which is very good for newly planted start-ups, is fairly miserable as a source of nourishment for this kind of sustained product-specific improvement. In Japan, the reverse is true. At Matsushita, for example, there is a commitment to being in the radio business. American firms wrote off radio years ago, calling it a dying industry. But Matsushita is married to it. To keep it attractive, they have had to develop first-class battery technology and so have developed a big business in batteries. They have done the same with the irons they make for home use. Not an exciting industry, but a good one nonetheless. A determination to innovate here—to create, for example, cordless irons (where the cord is attached to the pedestal base) and cassette steam irons (where the water is not added directly to the iron but to a detachable container)—has turned a sluggish $15 million business into a dynamic operation that accounts for roughly $500 million a year. Japanese soil makes this kind of focused commitment possible—and necessary.

In Japan corporations do not really believe that most products have a finite life. They believe they can always improve them and rekindle demand—and that they have to do so. Take the unglamorous toilet seat, for example. By most standards, it is not exactly a sexy product in a high-growth industry. But TOTO has added a heater to these seats so that they will not be uncomfortably cold when you sit down on them in winter. And then it added a microprocessor-driven bidet right in the toilet bench itself. These are high value-added additions. A normal toilet bench in Japan sells for roughly 50,000 yen. This new heated and microprocessor-driven product, called the Washlette by TOTO, sells for 160,000 yen and has become standard all over Japan. It is a huge success. The French have sat on the same old bidet for a century. Ten years of sitting on the Western-style bench gave TOTO a bright new idea initially, for patients with piles, and for everyone now.

You have to be in love with the toilet bench as a product to see the opportunity and to believe it worthwhile to follow. Too many American managers would have taken one look at the business, written it off as a declining industry, and tried to unload it as fast as possible. You can imagine the snickers on Wall Street when earnings suffer because of bidet R&D. American soil today does not provide the companies that grow in it any real resilience in the face of early signs of decline or decay. There is no staying power, no determination to find a way to innovate and add value. As soon as markets go soft, the culture says sell, get the value out while you can.

This was not always the case. It was not always so easy for Americans to sell off their businesses. In fact, their historical tradition, like that of the Japanese today, used to be to make the best of what they had, to pour their last drop of sweat into it, to hang onto it for dear life. Thomas Edison's famous dictum— "Innovation is 1 percent inspiration and 99 percent perspiration"—really used to mean something. It described what people believed and how they acted. No more. Under ever-increasing pressure from stockholders, many American companies have lost that vision. They have become traders of assets, not long-term builders of value. They create and then they move on. I don't understand this. I admire their creative ability, of course, but not the way they allow whole industries to disappear. This makes no sense to me, particularly in today's global environment where long-term success requires an especially steady hand.

I also reject the notion of a company being owned and possessed solely by its stockholders. A corporation is a social institution whose responsibilities extend far beyond the well-being of the equity owners to giving security and a good life to its employees, dealers, customers, vendors, and subcontractors. Their whole life hinges on the well-being of the corporation. Stockholders are only one of many stakeholders. When we address this issue of (declining) American industrial prowess, we have to ask what we mean by a corporation. When capitalism seems to be toasting victory over communism, the internal decay of capitalism in itself is ironic. But it need not be that way, if our greed can be contained. I believe this is particularly a good time to ask the fundamental question of what is a corporation. If a corporation's social responsibility to its people gives it more resilience and staying power, we need to review the greed-driven stock market mechanisms we have seen these past several years.

A Steady Hand

There is, unfortunately, much in the American soil that undermines the kind of steadiness global cultivation requires. The legal system in the United States, for example, is a wonderful mechanism for spoiling the soil for business. The Sherman Act says you cannot talk to your competitors about pricing. The Robinson-Patman Act says that your prices must be reasonably—and demonstrably—close to whomever you sell, sometimes to competing channels. So if you sell your products under your own brand and through an original equipment manufacturer, or as a private brand (a common practice in developed economies), you practically need ESP to be able to price your products without a grand jury taking interest. You have to shoot for a fairly narrow target zone without having any idea where the zone really is.

"Dumping" is another anachronism in an age when currencies fluctuate regularly and unpredictably. Whatever the legislative merit and intent of antidumping legislation, in practice it means that every time exchange rates fluctuate, foreign producers must flip around their prices like a yo-yo. Marking items up or down by 50 percent or 100 percent—and for reasons that have nothing to do with customers and everything to do with government shortsightedness—is a good way to confuse and alienate the public. Refusal to go along with this nonsense is likely to bring a headline-grabbing charge of dumping.

Global companies that are in markets for the long haul have to prepare to absorb these fluctuations themselves. From their customers' point of view, they must keep their product offerings on an even keel. But the legal system gets in the way. Most legal systems are created in a national economy and not in the borderless economy. After a point, managers are likely to throw up their hands and say, "Why bother? It's easier to stick to our own currency and our own markets." This may be no more than grandstanding, but it does influence decisions down the line. It gives indirect support to the impulse to cut and run when things get tough.

Consider what happened with Japanese auto and consumer electronics companies during the mid-1980s. They made enormous profits in the United States, some profits in Japan, but very little in Europe. An American security analyst looking at "segment-wise accounting" might have argued that Europe was not a worthwhile market, Japan was only minimally compelling, and therefore the company should pull out of both. Now look forward a couple of years. Different markets are booming. Currency exchange rates are greatly altered. Profits in Japan are soaring, but they have plummeted in the United States. Europe is significantly more attractive. What now? Pull out of the American market too? What's left? Nothing.

Being a global player means viewing the whole ILE as your proper soil, your place to plant and nourish your own distinctive businesses. No matter what happens to a particular product or region, you do not even think about transplanting the rest—not if the soil is right and the weather is mostly fine. They will bear fruit in another season, if not this year.

Today prestigious global companies are making good profits in Japan because they did not pull out when things were going badly there four or five years ago. They are doing well in Europe for the same reason. And they are doing okay in the United States. They have not been taken over by the stockholder logic run amok that has convinced so many American managers that the ideal global company has no plant, no facilities, no overhead—just one person in a room overseeing billions of dollars invested with a bunch of portfolio managers. Like the best companies everywhere, they have gardened with a steady hand.

Epilogue

Can all this be true? Will multinational companies all behave like model global citizens? Are national borders really disappearing? Will MITI and the Fed eventually learn to take a backseat in guiding the affairs of a single interlinked economy? Will developing countries catch up with the West and Far East by opening their borders?

We're not there yet. Many companies are still dominated by a headquarters mentality, myopically focused on the markets close to them and dominated by one nationality. Borders still matter and markets are still protected. Central banks still transfer millions of dollars of taxpayers' money into the hands of speculators by buying and selling currencies. Brazil and India still are isolated economies, despite their politicians' promises.

But we've learned a lot. Japanese companies, forced to set up production in the United States, are now committed to it. They will denationalize as a result. American manufacturers have revived their capabilities because of these transplants. They've focused on their workers again instead of battling with union leaders and suppliers. And every day the information age makes consumers, both individual and industrial, smarter and more demanding, not just about products but about policy. They're not likely to fall for the next round of "dumping" charges or arguments based on Japan's "poor island" mentality because they recognize what it costs them. A Japanese executive's wife told me recently that the United States Trade Representative Carla Hills, in her TV appearance in Tokyo, made more sense to her than any Japanese politician. Anecdotal evidence, but a sign of changes to come.

The interlinked economy is not yet a reality. Only parts of it have been linked. Money has become unregulated and moves around the world instantaneously. But not all assets do yet. Jobs are still hard to transfer.

Nevertheless, recognition of the growing interlinkage is increasing. On December 7, 1989, a *Wall Street Journal* editorial stated that it is time

> to recognize how integrated the world economy already is—not merely within Europe but at least through the developed world as recorded by the Organization for Economic Co-Operation and Development. In particular, we were struck by . . . two charts in a recent issue of the OECD Observer. They show remarkably similar trends throughout the OECD countries in two bellwethers of fiscal policy, public expenditure and public debt as a percentage of output.

As facts like this become better known, we can hope that government leaders will recognize that their role is to provide a steady *and small* hand, not to interfere. As the *Journal* noted, they will be

> "useful whenever economic policy makers get puffed up with their own importance and forget how intricately interdependent we are today. The graphs illustrate that at a basic level, supposedly independent Western fiscal policies have yielded results that mirror one another. This is going to be deflating to finance ministers who like to think of themselves as independent titans, leaving their thumbprint on their national economies."

Even France has had to back off its socialist aspirations. People there and all around the world have demanded it.

There is still fear of foreign investment and ownership. A few days after the *Journal's* editorial, *The New York Times* ran a front-page article on the purchase of an American manufacturer of semiconductor equipment by a Japanese company. Most of these sales "distress the nation," it said. Only at the end, buried back on page 44, did it quote the president of another American company in the industry that had been acquired: "Instead of layoffs . . . they gave everyone an extra week's pay . . . and said to me, 'You have unlimited capital.'" Despite the track record of Japanese investment and management in the United States, the distrust will die hard.

No, we are not one big happy family in the world yet, but the ILE may be closer than we think. For many of us, it's a case of shifting paradigms. We need to throw out Ptolemaic, nation-based models with which we interpret the world's events. Maybe that won't be so hard. For four years now, my family and I have spent at least part of the summer on Vancouver Island off the western coast of Canada. During the first three of those summers, we did not venture any significant distance outside Victoria, where our house is. Vancouver Island is a fairly deserted place, and it seemed to us that getting anywhere interesting would take more time than it was worth. Each year, though, I would hear reports about a lovely spot called Campbell River much farther up the coast—gorgeous scenery, wonderful salmon fishing. I was tempted, but I shrugged the temptation away. I didn't want to waste any of our all-too-brief time together by subjecting my wife and kids to a long, maybe boring drive through empty countryside to an unknown destination in the mere hope that the rumors about it were true.

Well, this past summer the stories about Campbell River sounded even better than before—so good, in fact, that I was determined at last to go and see for myself. So we packed for an expedition, piled into the car, and set off in the general direction of the river.

We didn't have a good map, and no one had been able to give us precise information about route or distance. On the one map I did have, it was not really possible to tell whether roads actually went where they seemed to be headed or just how good they were. So I'd estimate. On a good highway, maybe it would take us something like three hours or so, but out here in western Canada, in unsettled land, who knew? Better plan on twelve hours at least and a few overnights along the way.

Every step along the way, the trip surprised us. Our drive up the coast was pleasant. We made our way from one small village to another following clear and accurate road signs. Nowhere did we drive through tiresome or unsettled landscape. It was delightful—and took us all of four hours. We were able to look around, get as familiar as we wanted with Campbell River, make a few side trips, catch a twelve-pound salmon, and be back at our favorite restaurant in Victoria in plenty of time for dinner the next day.

Once we decided to make the trip, we found that it was already familiar to us—even though we had not known it at the time. No feature of the landscape we crossed was alien; no pattern of settlement starkly different from what we had grown accustomed to during our previous summers in Canada. We had language for it and mental labels that we could attach to it. Having finally broken the inertia, the resistance to leaving Victoria and looking farther north, we found that the only thing that had kept us from knowing the pleasures of Northern Vancouver Island sooner was our own reluctance.

In much the same way, many managers are still reluctant to explore the industrial landscape defined by today's emerging interlinked economy. It intrigues them, but they are wary. They have heard rumors about it. They have even felt its effects and been buffeted about by the forces at work in it. They may even have sought out primitive maps and made back-of-the-envelope guesses about what it might mean for them and their companies. But they have not piled the family into the car and set off to find out for themselves.

This book is meant to encourage them to make the trip as well as to guide them on their way. It is more than time that they go. The geography of the borderless world is "out there"—in the daily play of forces and activities and decisions around the Triad. It is real, for customers and for companies. And managers have to see this economy themselves. No armchair comments from experts. They must make the trip for themselves. And they must have the vision to understand what it is they have seen.

Besides managers, there are many others we should encourage to take the trip to a Campbell River: those delegates to G7 meetings who ask for "economic coordination" in order to preserve what little economic autonomy they have left in their countries; those bureaucrats who miscount trade figures month after month; the central bankers who pour millions into the pockets of speculators; the Ishiharas and Gephardts who would pit nation against nation; all those who would deny man his sovereignty as consumer, producer, and inventor in the name of ideology or in the pursuit of power. Man's role in the ILE is to create, imagine, and dream, and no government has a right to deny that.

If I had my way, I'd pay a third of all my taxes to an international fund dedicated to solving world problems, such as the environment and famine. A third to my community, where my children are educated and my family lives. And then a last third to my country, which each year does less and less for me in terms of security or well-being and instead subsidizes special interests. I'd be very happy to start paying these taxes after a group of leading nations adopted a mission statement, a "Declaration of Interdependence,"* aimed at the year 2005, and started working on the coordination necessary to force themselves to follow a mutually agreed on vision. Given the experience of Europe '92, 15 years is just enough time to get our act together—not too far away so it would seem to be our children's responsibility and not too soon to be unworkable.

Is that an idealistic, unrealizable aspiration? I don't think so. The developments and forces at work I've described in this book are powerful and will topple individuals, companies, and governments that oppose them. At their center is the oversupply of industrial and primary resources due to the dispersion of technology. The half-lives of monopolies and other market interferences will continue to grow shorter and shorter. These developments and forces may bring their own problems, but they will also bring a better life for all of us.

*See following page.

In recent decades we have watched the free flow of ideas, individuals, investments, and industries grow into an organic bond among developed economies. Not only are traditionally traded goods and securities freely exchanged in the interlinked economy, but so too are such crucial assets as land, companies, software, commercial rights (patents, memberships, and brands), art objects, and expertise.

Inevitably, the emergence of the interlinked economy brings with it an erosion of national sovereignty as the power of information directly touches local communities; academic, professional, and social institutions; corporations; and individuals. It is this borderless world that will give participating economies the capacity for boundless prosperity.

We avow that the security of humankind's social and economic institutions lies no longer in superpower deterrence but is rather to be found in the weave of economic and intellectual interdependence of nations.

As such, we believe that the interlinked economy

- Enhances the well-being of individuals and institutions.
- Stands open to all who wish to participate in it, mainly through deregulation of trade.
- Creates no absolute losers nor winners, as market mechanisms adjust participating nations' competitiveness rather fairly through currency exchange rates and employment.

Accordingly, the role of central governments must change, so as to

- Allow individuals access to the best and cheapest goods and services from anywhere in the world.
- Help corporations provide stable and rewarding jobs anywhere in the world regardless of the corporation's national identity.
- Coordinate activities with other governments to minimize conflicts arising from narrow interests.

- Avoid abrupt changes in economic and social fundamentals.

The leading nations must be united under this belief, so that they collectively can

- Enhance networking of individuals, institutions, and communities across the borders.
- Develop a new framework to deal collectively with traditionally parochial affairs, such as tax; standards and codes; and laws governing mobility of tradable goods, services, and assets.
- Induce developing, newly industrialized, and developed nations to actively participate in the global economy.
- Address and resolve issues that belong to the global community, such as:

Enhancement of the earth's environmental improvement and conservation of natural resources.
Underdeveloped nations.
Human rights and dignity.

Drafted by
Kenichi Ohmae (of Japan),
Herbert Henzler (of West Germany), and
Fred Gluck (of U.S.A.) of McKinsey &
Company
for a conference on trade and competitiveness
held in New York City, February 8, 1990*

*Fred Gluck is the Managing Director of McKinsey & Company, Inc. worldwide and Herb Henzler is Managing Director in Germany. We have worked together for 18 years. This statement, the product of many dinner conversations and debates, is one we each embrace and believe to be the best possible course for all countries and governments to follow.

Index

About the Author

No one understands better how Japanese companies operate than Kenichi Ohmae. Over the last decade he has helped some of the most well known and successful companies in Japan capture markets there as well as overseas. According to the *Financial Times* of London, Ohmae is "Japan's only management guru." He is by far the leading writer on business and management in Japan. All of his books (now over 30) are best sellers.

Ohmae's influence in the United States has increased substantially since his first book in English, *The Mind of the Strategist*, was published in 1982. As a senior partner of McKinsey & Company, Inc, an international management consulting firm, Ohmae has worked closely with the top management of several United States and European-based multinationals, helping them to develop new strategies and products, and to change their organizations so that they behave and operate as internationals rather than multi-locals.

In recent years, Ohmae has focused on social and political as well as management issues. He has, for example, attacked Japan's powerful rice and beef lobbies, calling for land reform. His most recent book in Japanese, another best seller, proposes a new constitution and reorganization of the Japanese government. In a 1989 poll of prominent Japanese, Ohmae was voted the country's most influential leader of public opinion.

In his books in English, *Triad Power* (1985) and *Beyond National Borders* (1987), Ohmae has begun to address not only the management problems of international business, but trade and other policy issues that divide the United States and Japan. As in his work with corporate clients, Ohmae has gained a reputation for taking controversial but fact-based points of view that have proved to be correct. His counsel is now sought by government leaders both in Japan and the United States.

Kenichi Ohmae was born in Japan in 1943. He is a graduate of Waseda University, The Tokyo Institute of Technology, and the Massachusetts Institute of Technology, from which he holds a Ph.D. in Nuclear Engineering. He makes his home in Tokyo. His travels, education, and work give Kenichi Ohmae a unique perspective in what he believes will be an increasingly borderless world.